Funny Money

Building Wealth in a System Rigged to Keep You Broke

By Justin Anderson

Published by RentSmart

ISBN 979-8-218-74214-0

First Edition

About the Author

Justin Anderson is the Chief Executive Officer of RentSmart.com, a SaaS company that provides tenant placement services for landlords and property managers. A licensed real estate broker in Georgia, Florida, and South Carolina, he also holds a Master's Degree in Finance from Harvard University. Over the past twenty-five years, he has bought, sold, and managed more than 2,000 units—from quiet single-family homes to lively multifamily communities.

In *Funny Money*, Justin trades buzzwords for plain English. He shows everyday people how a few simple real estate investments can break you free from the system rigged to keep you broke, allowing you to buy back your time, and create real options in your life. Readers appreciate his honest story, his willingness to share real life examples, and his focus on investing in properties that outlast hot markets.

At RentSmart.com, Justin leads business and product development with the same operator's mindset he brought to the investing field, helping customers simplify the hardest part of land lording—finding the right tenant. As a mentor to property owners and operators, he believes building wealth is a team sport, and the real win isn't just the cash flow—it's who you become while building it.

For Carrie, Courtney and Scott.
All of this was only possible because of you.

Table of Contents

Introduction

It was 11:45 p.m. The apartment that was nearly ready just 5 minutes ago, was now destroyed. Water was everywhere.

I had been running since 5:00 a.m. that morning. The kind of day where your phone never stops buzzing, your to-do list gets longer instead of shorter, and every small task feels like it might break you. I'd already missed my son's soccer game. I hadn't seen my wife since breakfast. She'd gone to bed hours ago. And here I was, standing in a newly-renovated apartment, alone, with a screwdriver in one hand and a thousand-yard stare in the other.

This was the final push. One last checklist before the tenant moved in tomorrow morning. I'd patched, painted, scrubbed, installed a new light fixture, touched up baseboards with a cheap paintbrush that kept shedding with every new stroke. The new carpet had been laid that afternoon. The place actually looked pretty good.

And then, just as I was about to call it a night, I heard it.

The toilet.

A faint but unmistakable trickle. The kind that means one of the inner components is failing. It wouldn't stop running. It needed new guts.

Good news: I had the parts in the truck.

Bad news: the shut-off valve under the toilet was stuck. I had been here before. There was no way I was turning that valve without completely breaking it off.

Now, any rational person might have walked away. Gotten some sleep. Come back in the morning, fresh and alert, to do it right.

But nope.

Not me.

I was in that perfect combination of exhausted and stubborn. The kind of tired that makes you feel invincible and hopeless at the same time. I had already invested an entire day into this place. I wasn't leaving without crossing that last task off the list.

So I made a decision. Maybe the worst one ever.

I decided to cut the pressurized water line to the toilet *without* shutting off the water to the building. Because—and this is where it gets good—I figured I could install the new valve fast enough to avoid any major mess.

You know, like a NASCAR pit crew. But for plumbing. Alone. At midnight. In a rental unit.

I convinced myself that if I moved quickly, maybe two, three seconds of water tops. A quick snip, a smooth shove of the new compression valve, and bam—plumbing hero.

Except that's not what happened.

As soon as I made the cut, the water line exploded.

11

It hit me square in the face like a firehose that was set to "destroy-everything-you-love" mode. The pressure knocked me backward, wrench flying, water roaring like Niagara Falls through a funnel. I scrambled to jam the new valve on, hands slipping, heart pounding, swearing like a man being mugged by his own ambition.

Spoiler alert: it didn't work.

Within seconds, water was pouring out of the bathroom like a busted dam. The brand-new carpet? Gone. The fresh baseboards? Toast. It surged through the bedroom like it had a mission, then rounded the corner and made a break for the living room. I had to find the water shut-off. I was soaked to the bone.

In desperation, I sprinted outside and dove headfirst into a holly bush, arms flailing, branches stabbing every exposed inch of skin, looking for the main line like a feral raccoon on a treasure hunt. I eventually found it. Shut off the water to the entire property. At 12:15 a.m.

The place was destroyed.

How did I find myself here? Slumped against the wall, dripping, defeated, holding a mangled valve in one hand and a half-crushed ego in the other.

This was supposed to be success, right? I was in the game. I hadn't just bought houses, I was an apartment mogul…at least in my own mind.

Unfortunately, the problem was much bigger than just one bad decision to hot swap a water supply valve. The real estate market was collapsing around me. We were entering the Great Recession, the worst real estate melt down in the history of our country. I had overleveraged into deals playing fast and loose, never once thinking the rocket ship of a real estate market would ever end.

And now I was paying the price. What had I done? What had I missed?

The Reset

A few days later, I found myself standing in line with my mentor ready to board a real estate investment cruise. It was branded as a floating mastermind for ambitious investors. Workshops by day, networking by night, exotic ports of call in between. On paper, it sounded like progress. Like the next rung up the ladder.

But deep down, I wasn't there to grow my business. I was there because I couldn't breathe.

That flooded apartment was the breaking point. I couldn't stop thinking about how hard I was working—how much I was sacrificing—and how little I had to show for it. I didn't need another seminar on spreadsheets. I needed perspective. I needed someone to explain how I'd built what looked like success from the outside, but felt like suffocation on the inside.

Our arrival in St. Thomas seemed perfectly timed to quiet my racing mind. The cove we were in looked almost fake—white sand, jagged cliffs, turquoise water so clear it felt filtered. The horizon sparkled with island silhouettes that looked like God had dropped a handful of jungle-covered gumdrops onto the sea.

The air smelled like salt and sunscreen and whatever peace was supposed to smell like…if I could just figure out how to inhale it.

I stood on that beach killing the vibe by whining to my mentor. Maybe I should just quit. Tuck my tail and walk—no runaway—to a new town. A city where no one knew who I was or cared. I didn't know how I was going to dig out of this situation. Maybe this giant dream of owning real estate was just an illusion. How could I be so stupid? What was I even doing here?

That's when my mentor delivered it. The existential gut punch I needed. No smile, no small talk—just that look, the kind that slices through your excuses before you even finish thinking them. He turned toward me, stopped just short of my sandy flip flops, and said: "You've been so focused on impressing everyone around you with how great you are that you've lost sight of what this game is really all about. What's really important."

He didn't stop there.

"It's all fake." he continued. "You've been measuring your success by how much money you earn, how fast you can earn it, how many hours you can outwork everyone else. The flashy car you drive, the big house. But you're chasing the wrong thing."

I swallowed hard, but said nothing.

"That's the rigged system. You are tricked into thinking money is the solution. You've bought into their game of more money equals more 'stuff'. And you deserve it, because that 'stuff' equals success. So, you trade your time—your life—to get more of it. You're so fully invested in it that you can't see it. You've figured out one piece of the puzzle, you bought some assets. That part is great, but you've completely missed the bigger picture." he said, "Money isn't the goal. And it certainly isn't wealth. It's a trap."

He leaned closer, "It's all a game…and you've been playing it all wrong."

Out of anger and driven by emotion, I opened my mouth to fire back, but he was already moving—grabbing his fins and heading toward the water with the breezy indifference of a man who just dropped a smoke bomb and vanished into the chaos.

I stood there for another second before flopping down into the sand, defeated, stunned and still vaguely offended, mentally defending myself. Unfortunately…or maybe fortunately… he was right. I was living in a trap. One I had actively built for myself.

I had a choice to make. Was this my breaking point? Or was I going to dig down deep enough and find what it took to pull myself out of this mess I had created?

As I sat there, surrounded by silence and the sea with just my thoughts, it eventually started to loosen. The warm sunlight held me like an exhale I didn't realize I'd been holding. It calmed me, and for the first time in days, maybe weeks, my brain didn't feel like it was trying to outrun something.

The sun was setting when my mentor finally walked back down the beach towards me. Not smug. Just present. I was still raw, but the edge was gone. Whatever heat I'd felt earlier had been cooled by the gentle breeze. That tropical island cove had done what no book, podcast, or seminar had ever managed to do: it made space.

"Look," he said, without ceremony, picking up right where he left off as we watched the waves lapping on the shore. "You've been working hard—no question. But there's so much you don't see yet. You've built a sizeable portfolio, at the expense of your life. You understand the details of the properties you bought, but you don't understand how the bigger cycles work, how markets shift, how money works, how its created, how it moves, how the game is actually played—and if you don't understand that, you don't stand a chance."

He leaned in and repeated it. "You're still playing the game like the money's the goal."

I stared at him.

"That's the big lie. That's the joke they're all in on—and you are the punchline paying with your life to earn it."

Silence.

"It's a rigged game, played with *Funny Money*. But if you know the rules, you can win. This is not the time to quit, or to have a pity party. This is the time to take action. To get your life and your business in order to prepare for the next cycle. There will never be a better time than now to do that. To stop chasing more money, and start building your life. Freedom is wealth. That is the goal."

There it was. The truth I had been looking for. Not that I'd been playing the wrong game—but that I'd been playing the right game in the wrong way.

I had been thinking freedom would show up once the numbers got big enough. But in that moment, it became crystal clear. Quitting the game wasn't the solution, and more wasn't better. I needed to learn how to build a better machine.

That's where the lessons resumed. But first, I should tell you how we got here…

Part I

Getting Started

Chapter One

The Game I Didn't Know Existed

The world isn't what you think it is. There's a game. You're allowed to play. But first, you have to see it.

Before the beach in St. Thomas…Before the rental checks showed up without me fixing up the properties…Before anyone called me an "investor" without snickering…

I was just a guy with a hammer.

And I don't mean that metaphorically.

I was a literal hammer-slinger. A framing crew grunt. The kind of guy who woke up before sunrise, smelled like sawdust by 7 a.m., and considered dry socks a luxury item. My job was to build other people's dreams—one two-by-four at a time—and at the end of every week, I'd cash my check, pay my bills, and maybe treat myself to the *fancy* Colby Jack cheese slices if things went well.

Nobody was calling that freedom.

Back then, if you'd asked me about financial independence, I would've assumed you were talking about trust fund babies or people who knew what "diversified holdings" meant. The closest I'd come to owning anything was the crescent-shaped bruise from my toolbelt and a half-punched Subway card.

But that was the guy who started this journey—not the one sipping Mai Tai's on a beach in the Caribbean.

That guy—*this* guy—took years to build. And he started right here: in steel-toed boots, dead broke, and absolutely clueless that there was even a game being played.

The Crack in the Foundation

I didn't hate construction.

I liked working with my hands. I liked the rhythm of the job—cutting, nailing, measuring, repeating. I liked the way a good framing crew could move like a pit crew, tossing up walls and sheathing like it was a well-rehearsed Broadway number, but with more cursing and fewer jazz hands.

And for a while, that was enough. At least it felt like progress. I was working. I was learning. I was side-by-side with my dad, working on his crew—a tough mix of tradesmen, veterans, and guys who drank their coffee black and their Gatorade warm. Good men. Calloused hands, tired eyes. Most of them older than me. All of them worn by the same routine.

What I didn't like was the future I saw in it.

It hit me one day on a job site. We were framing a two-story house, blue sky overhead, compressor hoses curling across the subfloor. I stopped to stretch my back, which was already letting me know it had beef with my life choices. And then I saw him—one of the older guys on the crew—limping across the gravel with that signature "I've-given-my-joints-to-the-trades" shuffle. And in that moment, I saw my whole life.

Not in some motivational-poster way. In a *terrifyingly literal* way. I saw me—older, slower, popping ibuprofen like Tic Tacs and praying my knees held out until I could pay off a used Ford.

Same limp. Same truck. Same story.

And I thought, *Hell no.*

Not out of pride. Not even out of ambition. Just out of raw, spine-deep survival instinct. I didn't know what the alternative was, but I knew it couldn't be this. Couldn't be the slow grind of physical labor into physical failure. Couldn't be framing someone else's dream while mine got buried under another layer of OSB and unpaid overtime.

That quiet realization didn't feel like a thunderclap or a burning bush moment. No angelic choir broke into song. It was more like a whisper in the back of my mind… but it wouldn't shut up. Something in me shifted. A small, stubborn gear clicked into place. *There has to be something else.*

That was the first crack in the foundation—the beginning of everything. I didn't have a plan, or a business model, or even a decent pair of shoes. But I had that crack. And once I saw it—once I realized the structure I was standing on doesn't go where I wanted it to—I couldn't unsee it.

The Book, the Burrito, and the Cheat Code

It wasn't announced by a booming voice in the sky or delivered by a financial angel in a three-piece suit. It came from a friend. A guy I barely knew, really. We were working on the same site and sat down to eat lunch together. Between nail pops and bites of our mystery meat food truck burritos, he handed me a book like it was a bag of leftovers.

24

"You oughta read this," he said.

I looked down at the cover. *Rich Dad Poor Dad.*

Now, let's be clear—I wasn't a reader back then. Not unless the book came with a toy in the box or had "menu" printed across the top. But something in his voice made me take it home.

I tossed it on the counter, next to unpaid bills and a stack of lumber receipts. It sat there for a few days, untouched. I was busy working, stressing, convincing myself that something would eventually change just because I wanted it to.

Then one night, after another long day of building someone else's future, I flipped it open. I wasn't on some enlightenment kick. I just couldn't sleep and there was nothing on TV. Just a few pages to say I tried it, I told myself. Give it ten pages before I doze off.

Then I hit the line. The one that lit an uncontrollable fire under me.

"Go buy a house and let someone else pay it off for you."

Wait…What? You can do that?

Like, legally?

I sat there staring at the page like it had just accused me of something. That single idea grabbed me and something shifted inside my head. I didn't doze off. Ten pages turned into thirty. Then fifty. Then I was sitting up in bed with the light on and my brow furrowed like I was trying to translate ancient scripture. Only it wasn't ancient scripture. The ideas were simple and straightforward.

I'd spent years working around houses—framing them, sweating in them, sweeping out sawdust and hauling plywood up stairs that weren't finished yet. But the idea that someone could *own* a house… and not live in it… and have someone else pay off the mortgage?

That idea had never crossed my mind.

Nobody had ever said those words around my dinner table. We weren't talking about assets. We were talking about electric bills and grocery coupons and which month the car tags were due.

I didn't know what any of it meant. I didn't know how buying a house even worked. I didn't know anyone who'd done it except people who *lived* in the house they bought. Landlords were characters in sitcoms. The whole thing felt like a dream someone else was having.

But still…That idea stuck to me like glitter at a kindergarten craft party. I couldn't shake it. Couldn't ignore it. Couldn't stop wondering how far behind I really was. I felt like I'd just been handed the cheat codes to a game I didn't even know I was losing.

The next morning, everything looked different. The jobsite, the nail gun, the piles of lumber—all of it suddenly felt like a set from a movie I didn't want to star in anymore.

What if this wasn't just something rich people did?
What if this wasn't a fantasy?
What if I could figure this out?

I didn't know the rules or the playbook. But now I knew the game existed—and I wasn't willing to keep pretending I was fine on the sidelines. Something had shifted.

Cannonball!

That book didn't give me a business plan. It didn't tell me what kind of loan to get, or how to talk to a seller, or what to do if the math didn't math. It did something worse—or better, depending on how you look at it. It lit a fire I couldn't ignore.

I tried. For a few days, I kept showing up on the job site like nothing had changed. Same coffee, same routine, same bent nails and busted knuckles. But that shift was real—real enough to make everything around me feel wrong-sized. The tape measure still worked. The nail gun still jammed. But I couldn't unsee what I'd read. Couldn't un-feel the itch.

I started to wonder: *What if I actually tried it?* What if I stopped just thinking about it or dreaming about "getting into real estate someday." What if this time it wasn't just another ad torn out of a magazine for a free seminar that I left on the fridge until the expiration date passed. I mean what if I actually tried. *What if I actually bought a house, rented it out and let someone else pay off the mortgage for me?*

The idea lodged itself so deep, I didn't just make a plan—I made a move. With the unearned confidence only a desperate, hopeful, and slightly naïve twenty-something-year-old can conjure, I didn't just jump, I cannonballed. Right into the deep end. No life jacket, no swimming lessons, and not even a snack for the journey.

Just me, my tool belt, a couple maxed-out credit cards, and a wife at home with two tiny kids who had no idea I was about to walk in the door with a grin and a crisis.

I quit my job.

Now, to be *extremely* clear: I do not recommend this path. This is not the part of the story where I become a role model. There is a much easier, less stressful path to win at this game—like keeping your job and just start looking at houses. Also, Pro Tip: Banks love people with paychecks.

But I didn't pause long enough to think about that. There's a kind of hunger that doesn't wait for logic. I didn't know what I was doing. I just knew I couldn't keep doing what I had been doing. I refused to end up like the old guy on my crew. And somehow, that felt like enough.

So, there I was. I didn't have a mentor. I didn't have a business card. I didn't even have a reliable truck. Truth is, I didn't have a clue. But I had a mental picture of a house. Not one I necessarily wanted to live in, but one I wanted someone else to live in—and I had this unshakable idea that if I could just find it, maybe I could change my trajectory.

So I chased it. I chased listings. Yard signs. Craigslist ads that smelled like desperation and expired carpet. I chased whispered leads from gas station cashiers and half-legible flyers stapled to telephone poles. If it had a roof and an address, I wanted to see it.

I didn't even know what I was looking for. But I knew I was looking. And more than once, I looked in the mirror and wondered if I'd completely lost my mind. There were nights I'd lay awake wondering if I'd bet the farm on a fantasy… and mornings I woke up thinking, *maybe I should just go back to swinging a hammer and calling it a day*.

But I kept going. Because deep down—*way* down, in the stubborn, scraped-up part of me that still believed—I knew that if I could just get that one deal… if I could just get the engine started, then maybe, just maybe, this thing could actually run. I needed to find someone to teach me. A mentor.

The Wrong Mentor – aka The Trunk Goblin

Somewhere between enthusiasm and delusion, I decided I needed to figure out how to play this game Kiyosaki kept talking about—*Cashflow*. He called it "a financial education in a box," and buddy, that sounded like exactly what I needed. I wasn't looking for an MBA. I just needed someone to hand me the decoder ring to this whole *go buy a house and let someone else pay it off for you* mystery.

Then I looked up the price.

Two. Hundred. Dollars.

In that moment, $200 may as well have been $2,000,000. We were living off credit cards and caffeinated hope. Groceries were a math equation. Diapers were a luxury item. And now here was this game—this magical plastic board of financial wisdom—dangling in front of me like a golden ticket I couldn't afford to scratch. That wasn't going to work. But maybe I could afford the next book in the series.

So, I went hunting at the local secondhand bookstore—all stale carpet, buzzing lights, and the faint smell of paper, dust, and unmet expectations. I found the finance section and started reading the back of the book like it might whisper instructions straight from the wealth gods.

That's when I felt it.

This guy—I kid you not—materialized behind me like he'd just stepped out of the "Suspicious Strangers" section of a mall security manual. One second I'm alone, and the next, he's right over my shoulder, breathing in my personal bubble like we were squished into a European elevator built for one.

"Hey," he whispers, in this creepy sort of hushed voice, "you like those books?"

I froze.

Like full-on statue mode. The man was so close I could smell the Starbucks double espresso on his teeth. I glanced sideways, trying not to flinch, half expecting him to offer me a black-market kidney.

"Uh… yeah?" I said, clutching the book like it might ward off evil.

"You gonna buy one?" he asked, eyes locked on *Cashflow Quadrant*.

"Maybe," I muttered, now inching down the aisle trying to get some space between us.

That's when he leaned in even closer—close enough to see the reflection of my poor decisions in his sunglasses—and said, "Don't buy it here. I've got it in my car. I'll sell it to you cheaper."

Wait… what?

Was this guy seriously slinging Rich Dad books out of the back of his trunk like they were hot mixtapes in 1985?

I laughed nervously, trying to keep it light in case he was dangerous *and* sensitive. "No thanks, man. I need a receipt."

He didn't miss a beat. "You got a napkin? I'll write you one." Like that was a totally reasonable solution.

That was my cue. I executed the kind of casual, high-alert bookstore exit you only see in spy thrillers—minus the tuxedo, plus a growing sense that I was being trailed by someone with multiple burner phones.

I started walking. Quickly.

He followed me.

Down the aisle. Past the endcap. Still pitching.

"You don't want the book? How about a DVD? I'll give you a *Rich Dad* DVD if you promise to watch it."

At this point, I just wanted this guy to get away from me so I nodded like a hostage negotiating release terms. "Sure," I said. "I'll take the DVD."

He lit up like he'd just won the lottery.

"Awesome," he grinned. "Follow me to my car."

Now, I probably should've said no. I probably should've done what any rational human would do when approached by a whispering stranger in a bookstore offering trunk treasures. But a free Rich Dad DVD? What if it had all the answers I was looking for? What if it changed everything for me?

He led me out into the parking lot, walking with the proud swagger of a man who definitely thought he was about to change my life— or sell me a counterfeit waffle iron. He stopped at this gold 1980s Mercedes, the kind of car where you open the trunk and half expect to find a portal to Narnia. And then boom—there it was.

A full blown disasterpiece.

It looked like a yard sale had gone feral. Boxes of who-knows-what, T-shirts with confusing slogans, a lava lamp, books, a George Foreman grill still in the box. Somewhere under the chaos, I half-expected a raccoon in a motivational speaker vest to poke its head out.

He rooted around through the clutter, muttering things like "I know it's in here somewhere" and "You're gonna love this one." Then,

31

finally, he emerged, triumphant, holding a DVD in a paper sleeve with his crumpled business card stapled on it.

"Watch this," he said, pressing it into my hand with the gravity of a wizard handing over a scroll that may or may not summon dragons—or bankruptcy.

I just nodded and stepped back trying not to make eye contact with him. But that's how desperate I was. I'd quit my job, emptied my bank account, and here I was hanging the dream of my financial future on a man who clearly thought toothpaste was a government tracking device.

And just like that, the man disappeared. Then it was just me, standing in the parking lot, holding a mystery DVD from a man I now only referred to as The Trunk Goblin.

What Was I Even Thinking?

The DVD didn't change everything. It didn't even make sense. I got home, popped it into the player like I was unlocking a secret, and immediately found myself watching a stadium full of people screaming like someone had just announced free Teslas and lifetime access to Costco. Lights flashed. Music pounded. And out came Robert Kiyosaki, strutting across the stage like a financial Mick Jagger.

For a moment, I was locked in. This was the guy. The book guy. The one who'd rearranged my brain a few months ago. But then things started to… shift.

He told his story—about going off-grid, self-publishing, selling books out of gas stations. So far, so good. But then names started dropping. Organizations. Product lines. The volume cranked up and the stage lights turned sideways, and before I knew it, I was watching what looked suspiciously like an Amway convention disguised as a TED Talk.

Something in my gut twisted.

Oh no…

I was being recruited.

The Trunk Goblin hadn't handed me wisdom. He'd handed me an MLM pitch. I turned off the TV and sat there, wondering if this whole real estate investing thing was just a shiny funnel for protein shakes and vitamin packs. For a split second, defeat set in hard. I thought about walking away again. Giving up. Just going back to the crew, picking up the nail gun, and calling this whole dream a weird mid-twenties life crisis.

No. Not yet. I couldn't do that. That wasn't the answer. Somewhere in the midst of the sparkle and stadium fog, I still desperately wanted to figure out how to buy a house that someone else would pay off for me. If I could do that, I believed it would lead to freedom and a life where I would never again have to chase a paycheck again. I still believed there was *something real* underneath it all. I just hadn't found the right person, the right mentor to explain it yet.

A few days later, poking around the Rich Dad website, I found an old-school message board with a thread called: Cashflow Circles. People who met up in living rooms and coffee shops to play the Cashflow board game. Not for fun. For learning.

What!?!? This was it! It was what I had been looking for. And one of the posts mentioned Augusta—my town. Just a short note: *Saturday mornings, 6 a.m. Cashflow game.*

The post was months old. Probably dead. Probably forgotten.

I replied anyway. *"Hey, you still playing? Still meeting? Please say yes."*

I waited. Checked the thread every few hours. Then every day. Nothing. Just silence and the creeping sense that I was the only person in town chasing this weird idea of financial freedom.

And then… a reply. They were still hosting the game. Still meeting on Saturdays. Still willing to let a stranger show up and play.

It should've felt like a win. But instead, I found myself staring at the message, trying to figure out how I was going to explain to my wife that I was getting up before dawn to meet someone from the internet to play a cartoon board game about rats and real estate…and by the way, it may all just be a hoax. A scam to recruit me into selling soap.

I wasn't sure what felt riskier: the idea itself… or how bad it might sound out loud.

A couple days later, my phone rang. It was the host of the game. We talked for a few minutes. Quick, easy, casual. Not a salesman. No DVD slinging Trunk Goblin vibes. No mention of supplements. Just a regular guy who, like me, had read a book and started pulling the thread. And just like that, hope crept back in. I wasn't alone anymore.

Meeting the Right Mentor

I pulled up just before six, fully expecting the gold Mercedes to be parked out front. My mind was still wrestling with the thought this might all just be a set up.

The house was dark except for a porch light and a faint glow in the front window. I sat in the truck for a minute, wondering if I had the wrong place…or worse, the right place but the wrong idea. Then I stepped out, walked up, and knocked.

The door opened almost immediately.

A guy, probably mid-forties, stood there holding a chipped coffee mug and looking like someone who'd already been up for a while. He gave me a once-over, smiled—the kind of smile that didn't overcommit—and invited me in.

The house was quiet. Lived-in. Not staged or sanitized. Just real. He motioned toward the dining table and went back into the kitchen like he'd done this a hundred times. I stood awkwardly for a moment, wondering if I was early or if this was the part where I get handed a mop and welcomed into a pyramid scheme.

"Hey!" I blurted, louder than I meant to—like a guy trying to casually defuse a bomb. "I've just gotta ask… are you trying to sell me soap?"

He stopped mid-pour, the coffee pot frozen in his hand. I knew it! He'd been caught mid-heist.

Slowly, he turned and looked at me. "…What?"

Don't "What?" me, I thought. Then I leaned in, dead serious.

"Are you trying to recruit me into Amway?"

Now it was silent. Just the soft gurgle of the coffee maker and my paranoia echoing across the room. He didn't blink. Didn't speak. He just looked at me super confused with his head twisted sort of sideways, the way your dog looks at you when it doesn't understand what you are saying. With total sincerity he replied, "Man, I have no idea what you're talking about."

We both chuckled a little. Me out of embarrassment. But he was sincere… thank goodness. No judgement. Just a calm confident energy about him.

This just might be real.

A few minutes later, others started trickling in. Friendly people, soft-spoken, casual in the way guys from the South can be without trying. They shook my hand and thanked me for joining them. But one thing was clear—the guy running this game was the one who answered the door when I got there.

He didn't lead. Didn't lecture. But when he spoke, people listened. He set up the board like a mechanic checking the oil. Everything in his posture said, *this matters*. And somehow, that made it matter to the rest of us too.

The game was amazing, colorful, and surprisingly uncomplicated. Cartoon rats. Career cards. Opportunity decks. On the surface, it felt like Monopoly's slightly cooler cousin. But there was something deeper at play, even if I couldn't quite put my finger on it.

We played. I fumbled my way through the turns, trying to make sense of the rules. Asked too many questions. Made a mess of the numbers. Tried to buy a boat with imaginary debt and got laughed at, kindly. No one made me feel dumb. They just explained, re-explained, and rolled dice when it was their turn.

And the guy who was running things—he kept watching. Not judging. Just tracking everything like he was seeing more than the rest of us were. He didn't say much that first time. But when someone asked about a deal, he weighed in. And when he did, the room went quiet for a beat. Not because he demanded it, but because *clarity* has a certain gravity.

I started watching him more than the cards. Trying to understand why he passed on a deal I thought was great. Why he seemed less interested in big wins and more interested in small, consistent moves. There was strategy there. Something layered beneath the cardboard and play money. Something I couldn't see yet, but badly wanted to.

Every Saturday after that, I showed up early. Sat at the table. Rolled the dice. Lost money. Made mistakes. Watched. Asked questions. I certainly didn't win very often. But I kept coming back because I could feel something shifting. A steady rewiring of my thinking was happening.

I didn't know it in those first few meetings, but that guy, the one who answered the door and invited me in…he was about to forever change the course of my life. He was about to become my own personal Yoda. My mentor.

Chapter Two

Fool's Gold

Not everything that shines is worth chasing. The first skill of an investor isn't finding gold—it's spotting the glitter that isn't.

In the first few weeks after finding the game, I started to see things more clearly, but I still didn't know what I was looking for.

Up to that point, my idea of "getting started" had mostly been desperation wrapped in action: chasing every listing I could find, walking random houses, talking to agents who smelled blood in the water. I had already quit my job, and the urgency was real. I had mouths to feed, bills that didn't care about ambition, and a growing sense that I was burning daylight.

I thought for sure if I just moved fast enough, hustled hard enough, I'd land a deal in a week. Maybe two. Something would shake loose. But every house I walked raised more questions than answers. I didn't know what I was looking at. Didn't know what made one property or neighborhood better than another. Couldn't tell the difference between opportunity and liability. I was operating on adrenaline and gut instinct, which—it turns out—are terrible tools for long-term investing.

The game and my newly formed friendships changed that. They gave me a framework. Sitting at that dining room table every

Saturday morning, I started to hear things I hadn't considered. How others talked about money and risk. How they spotted opportunity. How they moved through decisions without flinching. Some players moved faster than others, sure—but everyone was playing full out. Everyone made progress. That was definitely the most powerful part. It built my belief. Not just that deals were possible—but that I could find one too.

I started noticing that when the game ended, people didn't hang around to debrief. They had places to be—projects to check on, houses to tour, tenants to meet. Saturday wasn't just game day. It was go time. The game was their warm-up. Their mental stretching before stepping into the real thing.

I started mirroring their actions—this time with a little more perspective. Still urgent, still hungry, but slightly more grounded. Every Saturday, out looking at deals, believing at any moment I would find my first one.

The Gold Prospector

Just a few weeks into this next phase of my journey, a friend of mine—the quiet kind, ex-military, always looked like he was thinking five moves ahead—invited me and my daughter to go prospecting.

For actual gold.

I thought it would be a fun experience for a day. A break from the stress and anxiety that was ever present. I certainly wasn't expecting a life altering revelation to hit me sitting ankle deep in a creek staring at rocks.

Now, to be clear, this wasn't some touristy thing with brochures and souvenir vials. This guy was serious. He had boots, maps, pans, and a favorite creek deep enough in the woods that GPS gave up halfway there. When he said "let's play in the dirt," he meant it with spiritual conviction.

My daughter was in grammar school at the time, still floating in that glitter-and-glue phase of life where everything was pink and sparkly and held together with lip gloss. The idea of digging around in a bug-infested creek bed for flakes of metal wasn't exactly on her weekend wish list.

So I made her a deal.

"Any gold you find, you keep."

That lit her up. She invited a friend, both of them dressed for what I can only assume they thought was some kind of wilderness-themed fashion show. Hair curled. Sneakers too clean. Matching shirts. The whole situation smelled like Bath & Body Works and misaligned expectations.

We drove out, winding through gravel and pine needles until the road vanished and the trees swallowed everything. The creek was quiet and cold, slicing through the woods like it had secrets to keep. My buddy set us up with pans and pointed to a stretch of water where he said the current was just right. I watched the girls tiptoe across the rocks like they were made of lava.

At first, they hated it. The water was too cold. The bugs too aggressive. The mud too muddy. They panned for maybe five minutes before declaring the entire hobby broken. My friend, patient as always, just smiled and kept swirling his pan like he had all the time in the world.

And then it happened.

Mid-twirl, somewhere between a fashion pirouette and an awkward hop across a slick boulder, my daughter's foot betrayed her. One slippery misstep, and splash—down she went, straight into the creek, arms flailing, pride soaked.

Her friend exploded in laughter. And just like that, something shifted. They let go.

Somewhere between the splash and the squealing, all the lip gloss and tiara energy evaporated. The creek transformed from a hostile environment filled with bugs and betrayal into a full-blown amusement park. They splashed. They screamed. They chased each other like caffeinated water sprites set loose from a glitter factory.

Suddenly, they weren't royalty anymore—they were wild-eyed explorers. Jungle adventurers. National Geographic's newest interns. The transformation was so complete, I half expected David Attenborough's voice to narrate from the bushes.

And now that they were soaked to the bone and laughing like hyenas, something magical happened: they were *ready to learn.*

They sprinted—*dripping*—back to my buddy, who stood by the creek bank like some serene, clean shaven sensei of sediment. Gone was the eye-rolling, the bug-swatting, the sarcastic pan-swishing. In its place was genuine curiosity.

My daughter knelt beside him and pointed to a patch of gravel like she was about to strike oil.

"Is this a good spot to dig?" she asked, water streaming from her elbows. "Is this where the gold is?"

He looked down at her, smiled that quiet mountain-man smile, and said, "Sure, that's as good a spot as any."

She squinted at him. Suspicious. Sharp. Like a detective who just noticed the suspect's story had a plot hole.

"But… how do you *know* the gold's there?" she asked, lowering her voice like this was the big secret, the hidden chapter of the prospector's playbook.

My friend didn't give long answers. He just showed them how to swirl the pan. How to let the heavy stuff settle. How to wait.

The more they watched, the more they understood that this wasn't about finding something shiny and screaming jackpot. It was about seeing the stuff that looked *almost* like gold—but wasn't. Fool's gold. Mica. Glittering flakes that caught the light and tricked the eye.

He told us about the first time he went prospecting—how everyone showed up with fancy gear and confidence, how they all ran to the best-looking spots and started scooping up anything that shimmered.

And how none of it was real.

"I think I found gold," my daughter practically shouted, excitement bubbling under the surface like a shaken soda can.

My buddy didn't even glance up. Didn't flinch. Didn't pause.

"That's not gold," he said flatly, like he was rejecting a bad pickup line.

My daughter frowned. "How do you know?"

"Because if you *think* it's gold," he said, "it's not. When it's gold… you'll *know*."

Excuse me? What kind of fortune cookie wisdom was that? "if you think it's gold, it's not"? Seriously? My daughter just stood there, pan in hand, blinking like she'd just been hit with some kind of Jedi mind trick.

Still, she didn't argue. She was annoyed, but she went back to work. For hours, she panned. Her little vial started to fill with tiny flakes—each one just sparkly enough to give her a rush of hope, like scratching a lottery ticket and seeing the first matching number.

Each flake was a maybe. A *could be.* A "surely this is it." But every time she checked? Same result.

"Not gold."

Eventually, she stopped asking. She just kept working, collecting little shiny flakes in her vial. And then—finally—after hours of looking at rocks in the creek bed, it happened.

There it was, nestled in the corner of her pan like it had been waiting for dramatic effect. A tiny little nugget. Not a shimmer. Not a flirtatious flicker of possibility. A *nugget.*

It didn't whisper like the others—it screamed. Bold. Bright. Undeniable. The kind of gleam that didn't ask for attention, it *commanded* it. It wasn't playing coy like all those flaky imposters. This thing sat there like a tiny, metallic linebacker—solid, heavy, and absolutely sure of itself.

She didn't ask this time.

She didn't need to.

She just walked over, opened her hand, and let the weight of it speak for itself. No words. Just that smug, golden smirk only a real nugget can give you.

My buddy looked down, saw it, and broke into a slow grin.

"Now *that's* gold."

And then he added, "Once you've looked at enough shiny rocks, it becomes easy to spot the ones that *aren't* gold. And when the real thing comes along… you won't have to ask."

Boom. Wisdom bomb. No sirens, no confetti—just truth, dropped casually like a mic at a prospector's poetry slam.

He didn't say it like a metaphor. He wasn't trying to teach me any big life lesson. But, given what I was going through it sure landed like one.

Because while I was out there trying to figure out this investing thing, walking houses I couldn't afford and reading books I barely understood, I was also seeing a whole lot of shimmer. Deals that looked good until you ran the numbers. Promises that fell apart the minute you scratched the surface. People selling dreams with nothing underneath but pressure and fine print.

And it made sense—that to spot something real, you had to see enough fakes first. You had to swirl the pan over and over again and look at a lot of rocks.

The girls didn't fund their retirements that day. Just a couple tiny flakes. Enough to put in a vial and tell stories about. But on the drive home, wet socks steaming on the floorboards, my daughter held that little vial up to the window and said, "You can't really tell what's the real thing 'til you've looked at enough rocks, huh?"

I smiled, nodded, and kept driving. I wasn't sure if she meant gold or life. Didn't really matter. I just needed to keep looking at rocks.

$25 and Total Clarity

It took me fourteen months to land my first deal.

That's not a typo. Fourteen months of gazing at rocks like a lovesick teenager. Walking neighborhoods until my shoes gave up on me. Running numbers that never seemed to work. Watching every promising lead vanish faster than a donut at a fire station. I wasn't sitting around waiting for opportunity to knock—I was banging on every door I could find. But the only thing showing up was self-doubt.

And self-doubt doesn't arrive like a wrecking ball. It seeps in—slow and subtle. One unanswered call. One agent who ghosts you. One more day you open your spreadsheet and realize the numbers still don't work. It starts as frustration. Then it becomes a question. Then, eventually, it starts whispering in the back of your head: Maybe this just isn't for you.

But I kept going. Kept showing up. Kept swirling the pan.

Then one Saturday, after spending the better part of the day chasing leads that dried up faster than a kiddie pool in the Mojave, I found myself driving home. Exhausted and borderline delusional from overanalyzing listings that smelled more like scams than deals.

That's when I passed a small real estate sales office. I'd driven past it a thousand times before without a second glance. But today? Today, the sign out front practically winked at me. "Investment Property Available," it said—like a siren singing sweet nothings to a cash-strapped sailor.

Something in me clicked. Or maybe cracked. Either way, I flipped a U-turn like I was auditioning for the Fast & the Financially Anxious, and rolled into the parking lot like destiny had a reserved spot with my name on it.

Inside, the place looked exactly how I imagined: fake plants, motivational posters, and the faint smell of coffee that had been reheated one too many times. A receptionist looked up and offered a practiced smile.

"Can I help you?" she drawled.

I cleared my throat and attempted my best impression of someone who wasn't dying inside.

"I'm an investor," I said, puffing up slightly like a nervous blowfish. "I'm interested in the property you've got listed out front."

She nodded, unfazed, and made a call to the back. A moment later, a man emerged, all buttoned-up confidence and easy charm. He introduced himself, shook my hand, and smiled.

"So, how long have you been investing?" he asked.

"About five years." I replied, "How long have you been an agent?"

"About five years." He said. We both smirked. We both knew.

The agent who came out to meet me was brand new. I didn't know it at the time, but he was on "floor duty," which is real estate's version of being the new kid asked to clean the toilets—a shift so undesirable it's reserved exclusively for brand-new agents and people being punished by their brokers. And what he probably knew was that my entire portfolio consisted of exactly zero properties and a stack of rejection letters thick enough to use as a doorstop.

We were both greener than a St. Patrick's Day smoothie… and somehow, it was perfect.

Because that's exactly who I needed. Not a jaded veteran with five assistants and a Bluetooth headset surgically attached to his skull. I needed someone still fueled by hope and caffeine, someone who hadn't yet learned all the reasons something "wouldn't work." He didn't ask for a pre-approval letter. He didn't demand a proof-of-funds statement. He didn't even flinch when I confidently said I was an investor, despite the fact I was sweating like I was in a sauna.

He just smiled, nodded, and said, "What kind of deals are you looking for?"

That was it. No interrogation. No raised eyebrow. Just belief. And a willingness to go hunting with me for something neither of us had caught before.

I was excited.
And terrified.

We hit the streets the next day like two treasure hunters with a map written in crayon. He printed out a thick stack of MLS listings—the kind you could use as a booster seat—and we started driving. House after house. Fifteen… twenty… maybe more. I turned each one down faster than a toddler rejecting vegetables.

"Too much work."
"Neighborhood feels sketchy."
"This one smells like a wet Band-Aid."
At one point, I rejected a house because the grass "looked judgmental."

But to his credit, he didn't flinch. He just listened. No pressure. No push. Just this quiet patience, like a lab technician watching a very confused rat navigate a maze made of bad decisions.

Every excuse I made? He filed it away. Like a human algorithm, he recalibrated. Learning what I wanted, what I didn't, and what weird things would trigger me into abandoning a house faster than a dog who just saw the bathtub.

Then we pulled up to a modest little 2-bed, 1-bath place on the south side of town. Plain as toast without butter. No fountain in the front yard. No velvet Elvis in the window. But it checked every single box I said I wanted.

That's when the fear hit me like a rogue wave at a sandcastle convention. Not a little hesitation. Not a flicker of caution. I mean full-blown, heart-pounding, knees-gone-soft, brain-on-fire panic. This was it. The moment I'd been pushing toward for over a year. And I was teetering at the edge of it—staring down the first real leap.

"I should call my mentor," I said, mostly to buy myself a moment… or a lifetime.

I pulled out my phone like it was a detonator, half-hoping he wouldn't answer. Maybe he was busy. Maybe he was out of town. Maybe—please, universe—he was in the middle of a haircut and couldn't possibly weigh in on my financial destiny.

He picked up on the second ring.

"Hey," I said, trying to sound casual while holding back a full-blown panic attack. "I've got a deal I'm looking at. Wanted to see if you'd be able to come take a look, but if you're busy, I totally get it. No pressure at all. Really."

I trailed off like a teenager asking for prom money, practically handing him a script that said *"Please decline politely and let me crawl back into my fear cave."*

He didn't take the bait.

"Heck yeah!" he said without missing a beat. "Where is it?"

I gave him the address, still thinking I had a few hours to emotionally unravel before he could get there.

"I'm just around the corner," he said. "Be there in five."

And that's when my stomach dropped like it had missed a step on a dark staircase.

Honestly, I wasn't expecting him to say yes. Not that fast. Not that enthusiastically. A big part of me was still hoping for a delay. Anything that would buy me a little more time to marinate in my panic and talk myself out of doing something bold.

But five minutes later, his truck rolled up like the cavalry arriving ahead of schedule. He hopped out, clipboard brain already engaged, and went straight into deal mode like he was disarming a bomb.

"How many bedrooms? Bathrooms? What's the rehab look like? What are they asking?"

I did my best to answer without sounding like I was actively having a stroke. My voice cracked. My math was fuzzy. I may have blacked out halfway through describing the water heater.

Then he paused, looked me dead in the eye, and said the sentence that punched my fear right in the throat.

"Man, this is a great deal. If you don't buy it… I will."

It was like someone reached into my brain and flipped the breaker switch back on.

Just like that, the fear lifted. The panic lost its grip. The little voice in my head that had been screaming *You're not ready!* got drowned out by one louder, calmer voice: *You've got this.*

Because if he—Yoda—my mentor, the guy whose footsteps I'd been following for months could look at that crooked little house and see something worth owning… then maybe I wasn't losing my mind. Maybe I wasn't making a mistake.

Maybe all I needed was someone else to believe in it before I could believe in it myself.

That little house. That tiny, crooked-toothed starter deal that nobody else even slowed down to look at. From the outside, it looked like the kind of place where dreams went to get tetanus. But I patched it up—some carpet, fresh paint, a couple of appliances that didn't require kicking to function—and got it rented out for $525 a month. Not exactly setting the world on fire, but it was occupied.

After the mortgage, taxes, and insurance, I was left with a grand total of… $25.

Twenty-five bucks.

Barely enough to cover lunch at a fast food joint if nobody ordered fries. It was the kind of return that would make most people throw their hands up and ask if they'd accidentally joined a charity instead of a wealth-building strategy.

I remember telling my mentor, half proud and half sheepish, expecting at least a raised eyebrow. Maybe a polite nod and a gentle "That's a start." But he didn't blink. He just smiled that knowing smile of his—the one that usually meant he saw something I didn't.

"That's a good deal," he said, without a hint of sarcasm.

I squinted like I was trying to read fine print in the dark. "It's twenty-five dollars a month," I said slowly, in case he missed a decimal somewhere.

He chuckled. "You're looking at the wrong number."

I stared at him like he'd just complimented my imaginary yacht.

"You're trying to feed your family with your first deal," he said. "That's not what this one is for."

I stopped talking, struggling to understand what he was saying.

"This one is to prove you can do it. To show yourself you can find it, fund it, fix it, and fill it. You don't need this house to make you rich. You need it to make you ready."

He stepped closer, voice steady, tone matter-of-fact—like he was explaining how to tie a shoe. "You earn the right to make big moves… by executing small ones first."

And there it was.

Not a pep talk. Not a lecture. Just truth, delivered like only he could.

I hadn't hit a payday. But I'd crossed a threshold. I'd done it. All of it. And that meant I could do it again. And again. And again.

That $25 wasn't profit.

It was proof.

Chapter Three

Build a Life, Not a Portfolio

The goal is not to build a trap for yourself that is fueled by ego and driven by measuring yourself up against other people. The goal is to build a life where you are in control.

That first deal didn't set me up for retirement, but it rewired my instincts. After months of chasing everything that glittered, I finally knew what gold looked like—and more importantly, what it didn't. I had learned to wait, to swirl the pan, to trust the weight of what was real.

But here's the thing about finding your first nugget: it doesn't make you patient. It makes you *hungry*. The kind of hungry that doesn't nibble—it devours. One deal in and I was already mentally buying a dozen more. I'd caught the scent of opportunity and turned into a bloodhound with an MLS listing sheet. I wasn't just ready for another bite—I was standing at the buffet with a fork in both hands and fire in my eyes. I had no idea what it would cost me. I just knew I wanted more.

One Deal at a Time

After that first deal, I was walking like I'd just discovered gravity. Head high, chest out, strutting through Home Depot like I owned the place. As if I'd just been knighted by the International Order of

Landlords. I had reached the mountaintop of $25-a-month cash flow, and I was ready to go build an empire. It didn't matter that the mountaintop was more of a gently sloped hill behind a Taco Bell. I'd made it. And I was convinced—no, destined—to scale it again. Fast.

So the next time I sat across from my mentor—I came in hot.

"I want to buy ten more," I said, like I was ordering extra fries. No hesitation. No doubt. Just pure, uncut ambition, sizzling like bacon on a cast iron skillet.

He didn't blink. Didn't even pause mid-sip. Just nodded slowly, set his cup down, and tilted his head like a seasoned mechanic listening to a strange knock in the engine.

"If you haven't learned to operate one property well," he said, "what makes you think two will run better?"

I nodded, like I got it.

I didn't get it.

I smiled, like it was good advice.

I had no intention of following it.

In my head, I was already off to the races—lining up lenders, mentally buying entire cul-de-sacs, imagining spreadsheets filled with rent rolls and rehab budgets and wildly optimistic appreciation projections, picturing myself at cocktail parties casually dropping phrases like "my portfolio."

That warning? That was for someone else. I'd graduated. Passed the test. First deal done—time to double down. That whole "one deal at a time" thing? That was for people who needed training wheels. People who test the water with their toe before jumping in.

Not me. I was ready.

I didn't buy ten houses.

I bought twenty.

In less than a year, I went from rookie to regional manager of my own self-inflicted chaos. I was buying everything I could get my hands on. If it had a roof and a rent check attached to it, I wanted it. My phone never stopped ringing. Tenants. Contractors. Realtors. My inbox looked like someone had thrown confetti made of PDFs. I kept a clean shirt in my truck and a tape measure on my belt— ready to go from crawlspace to closing table at a moment's notice.

I was orbiting. And for a while…it felt amazing.

Every deal was a rush. Every closing was a shot of validation. I was growing fast. Building something big. People started noticing. Asking questions. Calling me an "investor" without the snicker.

Fast. Furious. Flawless.

Until it wasn't.

At first, the problems showed up like uninvited relatives—subtle, polite, easy to ignore. A missed call here. A delayed paint job there. But then they multiplied.

I hadn't learned how to screen tenants the right way. How to walk a job site and catch the things that would cost me later. I hadn't built systems. I hadn't built discipline. I hadn't built anything, really—just momentum, duct-taped together with ambition and a rolling line of credit.

The first deal had been proof of concept. What I needed next was mastery. But I skipped that part. I went straight to gobbling up as many deals as I could find. And now it was chewing me up like a dollar-store blender trying to crush ice.

So one day, worn out from a week of disasters I couldn't even joke about yet, I drove to meet my mentor. I sat across from him and finally said the words I hadn't wanted to admit:

"I'm overwhelmed."

He didn't gloat. Didn't smirk. Didn't lean back and bask in an "I told you so" moment. He just leaned forward, quiet and focused, and said:

"You need to slow down. When a man with money meets a man with knowledge…the man with the knowledge usually leaves with the money."

And it hit me—I hadn't just been losing money. I had been handing it away, gift-wrapped, to people who knew more than I did.

Plumbers. Contractors. Tenants. Agents. City inspectors. You name it. They weren't villains. They were just better prepared with more knowledge. I was the guy who brought a kazoo to a fencing match. And the only way out of it wasn't more speed… it was more skill.

I needed knowledge.

He wasn't trying to slow me down because he didn't believe in me.

He was trying to protect me—from the tuition cost of the School of Hard Knocks. Because when you're going fast, every bump becomes a crater. Every mistake turns into a budget-eating monster. Every oversight becomes a five-figure fire drill. When you're moving fast, little problems don't stay little. They grow teeth.

"The goal isn't just to own more," he said. "It's to learn more. And the slower you go, the cheaper the lessons."

I heard the words. I even nodded like I understood. But in my head, I was still picturing spreadsheets. Growth charts. I needed knowledge and I figured the best way to get it was by Empire-building.

Get Rid of the Measuring Stick

By the end of that first year, I wasn't just dabbling in real estate—I was starting to believe I was building something real. Tangible. Solid.

I had momentum. I had leverage. I had twenty-something rental doors and a growing stack of property deeds that made me feel like I was starring in my own version of *Million Dollar Investor: Small Town Edition*.

I wasn't just learning anymore—I was *doing*. Making moves. Signing contracts. Getting callbacks from bankers who used to pretend my voicemails didn't exist. Listing agents started saying things like, "Oh yeah, I've heard of you." And I pretended like that wasn't the best thing I'd heard all week.

Truthfully? I was eating it up.

There was something addictive about it all. Every deal I closed felt like strapping on another piece of armor. Like I was leveling up in a game I had barely known how to play a year earlier.

And the truth is, I liked how it felt. I liked walking into investor meetups with a little more weight in my step. I wasn't the wide-eyed rookie hugging the snack table anymore—I was starting to hold my own.

For a guy who used to spend his days swinging a hammer and praying the debit card wouldn't get declined, that shift hit deep. It was new territory. I didn't grow up around people who owned properties or talked about cashflow over coffee. My measuring stick had always been survival—make the payment, keep the lights on, try not to bounce anything.

Now, all of a sudden, I had something to measure.

And that's when the danger crept in.

Because as soon as you start measuring… you start comparing.

And comparison is a sneaky little thief. It'll steal your peace, your confidence, and your perspective—all while smiling politely and asking how many units you've got now.

People started asking questions. My name started getting passed around like a hot stock tip. I'd get invited to coffee or lunch by other investors—half of them curious, the other half hoping I might accidentally spill a secret formula between bites of my sandwich.

And I liked it. Not just the attention, but the *validation*. After years of pushing, learning, swinging hammers, and scraping together enough capital to make a deal work, people finally wanted to know what *I* was doing. I wasn't chasing conversations anymore—they were chasing me.

I started walking into rooms with a little more weight in my step. Not arrogance, exactly. But something close enough to confuse a humble man.

And that's when I picked it up—the measuring stick.

I didn't mean to. I didn't even notice it at first. But somewhere between the investor meetups, the weekend seminars, and the strategy sessions over gas station coffee, I caught myself keeping score.

How many units do I have?
How many flips are in the pipeline?
How many markets am I in?

It was everywhere. Lingering in conversations. Hiding in the pauses between sentences. People didn't always say it outright, but it was baked into the culture. A quiet, competitive undercurrent. An unspoken contest.

And without realizing it... I was in it.

At first, it was subtle—like a leaky faucet of comparison dripping in the back of my brain. Just a glance at someone else's portfolio here, a sideways comment there. Nothing dramatic. But over time, it got louder. It crept into my decision-making like kudzu, wrapping itself around my priorities until I couldn't tell the difference between a good deal and a loud one.

I said yes to properties that didn't quite fit the model. Took on projects that looked great on paper but felt like a migraine in real life. Started swinging for the fences, not because the pitch was right—but because I wanted people to *see* me hit something.

I wasn't chasing value anymore. I was chasing volume. And I told myself it was ambition. Hustle. Vision. Words that sound noble until you realize you're just dressing your ego in a business suit.

But underneath all of it, I was trying to prove something.

To my wife—that the late nights and early mornings were worth it.

To my mentor—that I'd absorbed the lessons, that I was *worthy* of the time he'd poured into me.

To the other guys in the room—that I belonged at the table.

And most of all... to myself.

Because somewhere along the line, I'd stopped building for freedom. I was building for validation.

Then came the barbecue lunch.

Hole-in-the-wall joint. Great brisket. Bad lighting. One of those places where the tables wobble unless you wedge a napkin under the leg.

I was mid-sandwich, rattling off the stats of a guy I'd just met at the local REIA meeting—same age as me, already sitting on 75 units across three markets, with a full-time staff and the kind of polished confidence you normally find in political candidates and cult leaders.

"He's really doing it," I said, practically narrating his resume. "It's wild how fast some of these guys scale."

My mentor nodded and took another bite of brisket like he was grading the spice rub. Then he looked up, calm as ever, and said:

"You chasing his outcome... or your own?"

I froze, sandwich halfway to my mouth.

He didn't press. Didn't raise his voice or launch into a speech. Just let the question sit there—like a puddle of hot BBQ sauce waiting for me to step in it.

"You don't know what his portfolio cost him," he added, setting his cup down. "Not what he *paid*. What it *cost*."

And he wasn't talking about purchase price. He was talking about the stuff no spreadsheet shows you: missed dinners, late nights, frayed nerves, maxed-out risk, waking up at 3 a.m. with your chest tight and your brain spinning like a bingo machine.

Then he leaned in a little, voice still soft, and said something that hit like a freight train wrapped in flannel:

"You say you want freedom. But are you building freedom…or just building noise?"

A perfectly landed black eye.

When I first started this journey, I wasn't confused about what I wanted. I wanted time. I wanted control. I wanted to be the dad who didn't miss the school play because drywall was behind schedule. The husband who could put his phone down at dinner— not just silence it, but *actually* let go of the day and be present. I wanted to go on a family vacation without praying the HVAC at unit 4B didn't explode while I was gone. I didn't need to be rich. I needed to breathe.

That was the dream.
Freedom.

But somewhere along the way, that pure desire—that clear, quiet picture of life on my terms—got tangled in a different kind of fuel. A louder kind. The kind pumped out in conference rooms, real estate podcasts, and group chats where deals are treated like trading cards.

Recognition.

Reputation.

Respect.

I started craving the applause that comes from performance, not just the peace that comes from alignment. The scoreboard changed, and with it, so did I. I wasn't just chasing freedom anymore. I was chasing *visibility*.

I started watching other people's numbers like they were mile markers on a race I didn't remember signing up for. Twenty doors. Thirty doors. Syndication. Multi-state expansion. The more I scrolled, the more I second-guessed. Should I be going faster? Am I behind? Is my pace too cautious? Is "slow and steady" just something we say when we're losing?

I wasn't asking if a deal made sense for *me*. I was asking if it would make me look like I was keeping up. And let me tell you, there's no worse investment filter than ego in a hurry.

The truth? The more I listened to those voices—the guys scaling faster, moving bigger, talking louder—the more I lost the thread of my own story.

I forgot what race I was running. And who I was running it for. That's the danger of the measuring stick. It never tells you what something's worth. It only tells you how it compares.

And if you're not careful, you'll spend years building someone else's dream, chasing someone else's scoreboard, trying to hit milestones you never even meant to aim for. All the while, drifting quietly, steadily, away from the life you *actually* wanted to build.

I started to feel it. It wasn't loud—not at first. Just a quiet gnawing at the edges of my drive. A faint tug every time I sat with another project that didn't quite fit, but still said yes to. A flicker of unease during the tenth conversation that week about "scaling" when I hadn't had a real moment of peace in months.

I was still working hard. Still doing deals. Still building. But I had lost the thread. And worse... I had stopped asking the most important question of all: *Why?*

What was I building?
What was it for?

If you'd asked me back then, I would've said all the right things. Freedom. Legacy. Passive income. Check, check, check.

But if you'd looked closer—if you could've peered into my calendar, my stress level, my home life, or the circles under my eyes—you might've seen the truth.

I was still a Sophomore. Smart enough to sound experienced, but not yet wise enough to slow down. Confident enough to make noise, but not quiet enough to listen. Hungry enough to hustle, but not grounded enough to rest.

The lesson hadn't landed yet. Not fully. It was still circling, waiting for the right moment to stick.

And that moment was coming.

Hard.

More is NOT Better

I kept hustling. A few years into my investing career, I was in the big leagues—or at least that's what it looked like on paper. I had gone from nervously closing on a $25-a-month rental to signing for a 100-unit apartment complex. A few years earlier, I had been swinging a hammer on other people's job sites. Now I was walking through brick buildings with a leasing office, a payroll, and a growing belief that I had figured it out.

The next couple of years were a blur. Deals kept coming. Banks kept saying yes. Lenders offered terms before I even asked for them. I scaled up fast. I ran crews, managed vendors, put systems in place—or so I told myself. I was operating over 350 units, and still saying yes to more.

My ego was in overdrive, I was invincible. I bought another 250 units, this time *out of town*. Not just another property—a whole new market. I was scaling now. Scaling—a word that made me feel so grown-up I half expected someone to start calling me "sir." I had property managers, leasing agents, a small battalion of maintenance guys who could rebuild an HVAC unit in their sleep. Some days I didn't even have to be there.

But the machine needed fuel. Constant fuel. Every decision became heavier. Every small issue had the potential to become a five-alarm fire. I found myself tethered to my phone—not by greed, but by gravity. There was always something pulling at me. A missed rent payment. A broken pipe. A vendor who didn't show up. A city inspector who found one more thing that suddenly had to be fixed.

And still, I pushed harder. Expanding. Growing. Scaling. Until I woke up one morning sitting on more than 800 doors.
Eight. Hundred.

It was the kind of number that makes people lean in at conferences. The kind of number that gets you introduced at events. People wanted to hear how I'd done it. I started getting asked to speak. I started answering questions I hadn't even asked myself yet. And the story I was telling—that I was building wealth, building freedom, building a legacy—felt true. At least it did on the surface.

But underneath, something else was happening. I was tired. This was not the kind of tired that goes away with a good night's sleep. A deeper kind. A slow erosion. Like something was being quietly drained. I would miss dinner because of a last-minute call. I would hear my kids laughing in the backyard and feel like a visitor in my own life. I told myself it was temporary. That this was the cost of building something that mattered. That I'd slow down soon—after the next deal, or the next refinance, or the next project.

But the goalposts kept moving. And so did I.

That's when I found myself sitting on that beach in St. Thomas, reeling from the existential gut punch delivered by my mentor. That was the moment I realized I wasn't in control anymore. The machine was running me. I had created a very sophisticated cage—one that looked impressive from the outside but left very little room to breathe.

And the worst part was, I had done it to myself.

So I did something that, to most people in this business, sounded like blasphemy. I began planning a multi-year unwind. I was going to start selling assets—shift away from the multifamily monster I had created and return to where it all started: single-family homes.

You know, the kind of houses that don't need a regional manager, a conference room, or a quarterly report with color-coded spreadsheets. The kind of homes most people "graduate" from.

But I wasn't chasing status anymore. I was chasing simplicity. I wanted control. Margin. Sanity. So, piece by piece, I sold off the portfolio.

Over time, I shrank my holdings by over 90%. I could breathe again. And then, the most incredible happened.

My cash flow didn't shrink—it grew. And not just by a little. It quadrupled. Which felt a bit like waking up to find out your garden gnome laid golden eggs while you were asleep.

At first, the math didn't make sense. How could fewer properties equal more income? How could scaling down create a bigger life? It was like the universe was running some kind of cosmic rebate program.

But then it clicked. That elusive truth my mentor had tried to tattoo on my brain years earlier—the one I'd nodded at but didn't really understand:

More is not better.

More units didn't mean more freedom. More leverage didn't mean more peace. More visibility didn't mean more clarity. Sometimes, more is just... heavier.

It's so easy to romanticize scale. To treat growth like gospel. To let your self-worth rise and fall with the number of doors you've collected like poker chips at a high-stakes table.

But the smartest investors I know? Guys like Yoda, my mentor. They don't just count what they own—they weigh it.

They ask better questions:

What's the real return on my time?
Does this deal serve my goals—or hijack my sanity?
Am I building something that adds peace... or pressure?

Looking back, I needed the chaos. I needed to sprint too fast, to juggle too many things, to nearly drown in my own success.
Because that's what it took for the lesson to land.
Not in theory—but in my bones.

It was never about owning more doors or chasing more zeroes. It was about alignment.

About designing a life that actually fits. About building a business that supports who you are—not one that eats you alive and calls it legacy.

Because real success?
It's not owning more.

It's owning your life.

Build a Life, Not Just a Portfolio

That day on the beach in St. Thomas, the existential gut punch moment from Yoda had left a mark. But in a good way.

The numbers said I was winning. More properties, more deals, more systems, more everything. If you judged by spreadsheets alone, I had built something impressive.

But I didn't feel successful. I felt cornered.

I had a keychain full of doors and no idea which one led to the life I actually wanted. Every unit came with a new responsibility. Every deal added pressure. I had started with a vision of freedom—mornings with my kids, dinners without interruptions, a business that served my life, not swallowed it. But somewhere along the way, I had traded that for motion. For volume. For a machine that only worked if I kept throwing my time into the furnace.

I told myself this was what growth looked like. That the stress was a sign I was doing something big. But sitting there in that moment, I realized something important:

I wasn't building a life.

I was just getting busier.

A few weeks after the cruise, I met my mentor for lunch at a diner that hadn't changed since vinyl booths were fashionable and where the coffee came scorched. I laid it all out—the plan to shrink my portfolio, to reduce my leverage, to buy my time back and be able to breathe.

He just listened, calm as always, until I finally ran out of words. Then he set down his fork, looked me square in the eye, and said: "Now you're getting it. More isn't better…it's just more. The purpose of business is not busy-ness. The purpose of business is to build a machine that generates cash flow without your direct day to day involvement. That is freedom."

That was it. That was the problem. I hadn't created freedom. I'd created obligation. A machine that demanded more—more input, more management, more me. And the worst part? I had built it with my own two hands, one well-intentioned deal at a time.

The lesson wasn't that growth is bad. My mentor wasn't anti-scale. He was allergic to systems that stole your life while pretending to build it—the kind we justify with big goals and bigger bank accounts, while quietly drifting from everything we said we wanted in the first place.

He wasn't telling me to stop building.

He was inviting me to build better.

To build with a filter—a way of knowing what fits and what doesn't. What to say yes to. What to walk away from. What to pursue not because it's available, but because it's aligned.

He gave me something I hadn't had in a long time: clarity. I had spent years chasing more—more deals, more growth, more noise. But the life I wanted? That required less. Less clutter. Less ego. Less motion for motion's sake. What it needed was design. Intention. A strategy. One built around my actual values—not just my ambitions.

As painful as it was to get here, my teachable spirit had returned. I was ready to learn. To understand the real estate cycles, and learn how money really worked.

Part II
The Three Lenses

Chapter Four

The Property Life Cycle

The Street Level View: A property isn't good or bad based on where it is in the cycle. What matters is that you know where it is—and what it will take to carry the investment through its life.

I had finally shaped my portfolio into something I could live with—lean enough to be manageable, strong enough to produce healthy profits. I'd spent the past year rebuilding not just my business model, but the way I thought about real estate altogether. No more ego-driven growth. No more chasing applause. Just intentional, thoughtful deals—aligned with the life I actually wanted to live.

I had room to think. Room to breathe. Room to look at an opportunity and ask if it made sense for my life as well as my numbers. I could say no without hesitation, and when the right kind of project came along, I could say yes without wondering if it would pull the whole operation off balance.

Real estate has a funny way of luring you in. Not with glittering spreadsheets or syndication hype, but with something far more tempting: a good story. And this one started, of all places, in the green room of a community theatre.

A Black Box Theatre and a Dream

We were hanging out backstage in the dressing room during a lunch break. My wife, ever the enthusiast for dragging me into artistic chaos, had roped me into performing in a local stage play. It was being performed for every school kid within a 40-mile radius who had a permission slip and a teacher who needed an excuse to avoid long division.

As we gnawed through ham sandwiches and half-baked plotlines, the conversation drifted, as these things do, from the script to something far more dramatic: the dream of growing the local theatre community. One of the actors leaned back and mused, "You know, I've always wanted to open a black box theatre…"

Cue dramatic lighting and swelling music.

The tech director chimed in, eyes glazed with vision and possibly exhaustion, adding, "Yeah, somewhere small but gritty—an Off-Broadway vibe."

That's when the second actor, never one to miss a cue, pointed at me mid-bite and declared, "You should get him involved! He's a real estate guy. He could buy the building!"

Suddenly, the spotlight was on me, mouth full, looking like a chipmunk caught shoplifting a granola bar.

And just like that…the idea was born.

I was instantly smitten. I loved the concept of owning a space that could serve both community and commerce. My wife was lit up about it, and after years of scaling down, I was finally in a place where I could choose deals based on fit, not volume.

All of it was catnip for my entrepreneurial brain.

We determined what kind of building we were looking for. It had to be in a decent location. Close enough to downtown's foot traffic to draw a crowd, but still priced within reach. This was going to be a theatre, and theatres aren't exactly known for fat profit margins, so every dollar counted. My wife wanted charm and character; I wanted a number that wouldn't keep me up at night. I had the rehab skills to take on a serious fixer-upper if the price made sense.

That was the voice in my head as we wandered downtown like a pack of theatre nerds on a treasure hunt. We weren't after gold doubloons—We were after a dream.

Then we saw it: a squat, slightly cranky-looking building that was practically whispering our names. In the window hung a sun-faded "FOR SALE" sign so old it might have been printed on a dot matrix printer. It looked like it had survived more than one battle— and possibly a small fire. But hey, this could be it.

I called the agent listed on the sign and asked about the price, bracing myself. He tossed it out casually, like it was pocket change. I nodded with confidence, but inside my brain was short-circuiting.

They want how much? For this?

The building wasn't just a fixer-upper—it was a fixer-upper's grandfather. A shell of a building sandwiched tightly between other boarded-up relics like forgotten teeth in downtown's once-proud smile. It had the aesthetic charm of skid row. The floors were completely rotted. Gaping holes the size of manhole covers yawned across the space like open mouths daring us to fall in. The only remnants of civilization were patches of faded black and white checkered sheet vinyl clinging to the subfloor.

And above us, the ceiling was a tragic multi-era mashup that told a story of poor decisions and water damage. Originally, it had been one of those charming old pressed tin ceilings—lovely in theory. But at some point, a roof leak had apparently turned that charm into a liability. Instead of fixing the leak, someone had MacGyvered the situation by hanging a layer of drop ceiling underneath it. And not just one…There were two.

Apparently, when the first layer failed to conceal the roof leaks—or the shame of ignoring them—the next best solution was to just install another layer. Out of sight, out of mind. I imagined the conversation: "Should we fix the leak?" "Nah, just hang more ceiling under it."

But, the location had promise—just a few blocks from the revitalization action, where coffee shops and local art galleries were popping up. The city's two other theatres were just a block away in the opposite direction, landing us in a perfect spot to expand the "theatre district".

That's when the agent asked if we would like to see the rest of the space?

I blinked. The rest? What else was there to see? We were standing in a giant echo chamber. Aside from the bathroom tucked into the back right corner and what looked like a small storage closet behind it, I could see straight through to the back door without taking a single step. There were no walls, no hallways, no hidden alcoves or secret passageways. Just exposed brick, bad flooring, and shattered dreams.

But the agent turned without explanation, walked out the front door and headed over to the corner building—and started unlocking it. Now I was confused.

I followed him, wondering if this was some kind of real estate magic trick. And that's when he dropped the twist: the listing wasn't just for the single building we had just "toured". It was for three buildings, side by side. This was getting interesting.

Three interconnected properties? The asking price was starting to seem reasonable. Still beat up, still boarded up, still missing chunks of ceiling and flooring—but it was half the block. And owning that much downtown real estate opened up an entirely different conversation.

A conversation I needed to have with my mentor.

Countertop University (CTU)

We met downtown at his office. Old shop building, worn carpet, dusty trophies in the windows. Dozens of invoices laid out across the counter. It was our usual spot when the questions got too big for a phone call. We called it Countertop University—CTU for short.

He pulled out a napkin, naturally. That was his preferred medium—cheap, disposable, and never too far from a decent cup of coffee. He drew a chart with a horizontal axis labeled time, and a vertical axis labeled value.

At the beginning of the timeline, he drew a line straight up and explained when a property is first built, the day it is completed it is at its highest value. From that day forward it begins to fade—to depreciate, he told me as he drew a sloping curve downwards on the chart. Time eventually gets everything.

He was sketching out what he called The Property Life Cycle—the P-cycle—the natural aging curve that every building goes through.

VALUE · **NEW BUILD** · *DEPRECIATES* · *TROUGH*

TIME

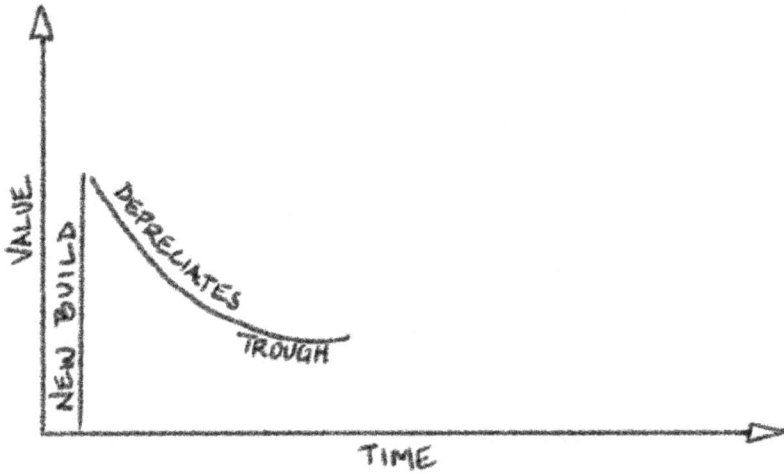

He explained how value is lost not just through physical decay, but through the way people live and work now. Neighborhoods shift. Industries change. Properties decline into the bottom of the trough. What once made sense stops making sense. If you don't know how to read that curve—where a property sits on it—you'll end up buying a corpse and calling it a bargain.

"But here's the good news," he said. "There is opportunity everywhere on the curve if you know what you are buying and plan properly for it."

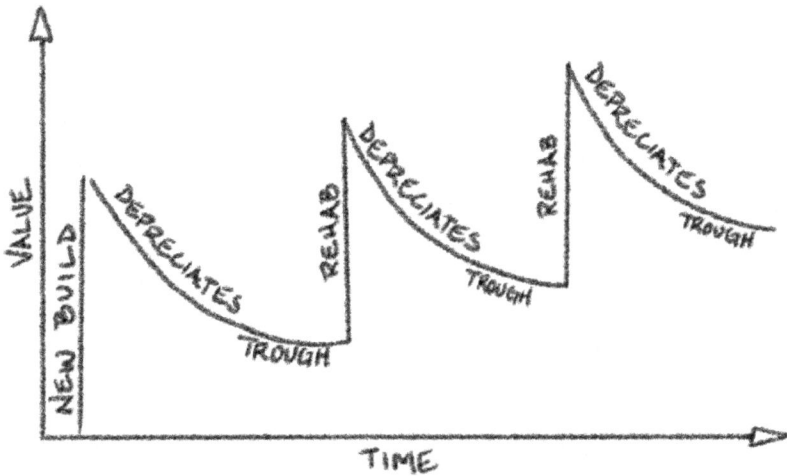

VALUE · **NEW BUILD** · *DEPRECIATES* · *TROUGH* · *REHAB* · *DEPRECIATES* · *TROUGH* · *REHAB* · *DEPRECIATES* · *TROUGH*

TIME

81

He grinned and drew a sharp vertical line shooting upward from the bottom of the curve. New use. New energy. New life.

Yoda paused and started tapping his drawing on each of the four phases. A new building, followed by a slow fade. Then the trough—when its tired and wrong for today. Then the reposition—new money, new use—back to prime.

Four Phases of the Property Life Cycle:

1. **New/Reset** (New build or full rehab)

2. **Depreciation** (Use & Fade begins)

3. **Trough** (Physical deterioration)

4. **Rehab/Reposition** (big ticket fixes+ new use) → **Stabilize** (back to prime)

When a property hits the bottom of its cycle, there can be real opportunity. If you have the eyes to see it, and the stomach and the budget to fix it, you can bring it back to life—better, stronger, and more aligned with what the neighborhood actually needs today.

This was amazing. It was a masterclass about how smart investors make their money not just by buying low, but by buying at the right moment in the cycle, with clarity.

That's what this building—these three buildings—were. Tired old warriors, waiting for someone to recognize their next purpose. As absurd as they looked from the outside, this property had everything. Strong bones. A dirt-cheap entry point. A vision aligned with the community. And best of all? It sat right in the path of progress—that slow, quiet wave of development that creeps in when no one's paying attention, reshaping neighborhoods block by block, until suddenly everyone wishes they had bought in five years earlier.

We weren't guessing. We were reading the signs. New sidewalks. Public art funding. Infrastructure upgrades. The theatre district was stirring, and this building was right in the middle of it.

The P-cycle Applied

We called the listing agent back to schedule a second viewing before writing an offer. That's when he gave me the backstory of the building—a history of the property's life. I started taking notes.

The buildings were originally constructed in the 1870s, by Citizens and Southern Bank. These buildings were in the heart of downtown, near all the other financial institutions of the day.

But by the early 1910s, Citizens had moved on. The buildings had seen better days, having run the full course of their useful life.

I flipped to a new page in my notebook and drew the chart with two perpendicular lines. Then started adding to it, creating an art piece of sorts.

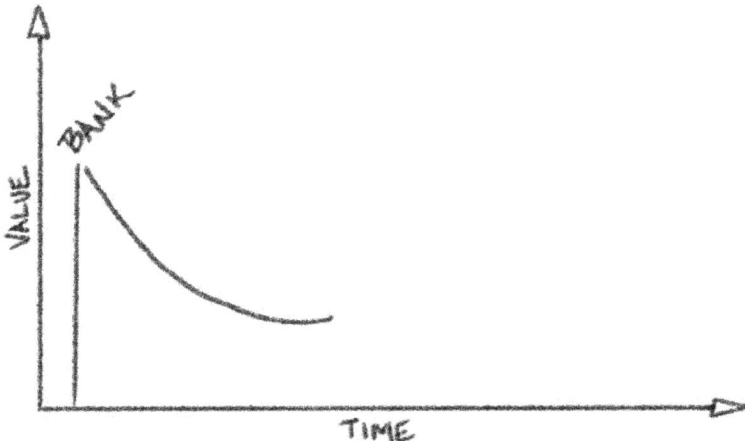

By the 1920s, renewed interest was cropping up in the area, and a jewelry shop took over the space. A complete restoration happened, bringing the property back up to a new high, both in value and in the use of the space.

I drew another vertical line up the chart. This time to an even higher value. Commerce was bustling downtown in the 1920s. It was the center of retail business in the city, long before indoor malls, or strip centers existed in the suburbs.

This run was good for awhile, but by the 1960s downtown was ready for its next face lift and revitalization effort. I drew another slow arcing curve back down near the bottom of the chart.

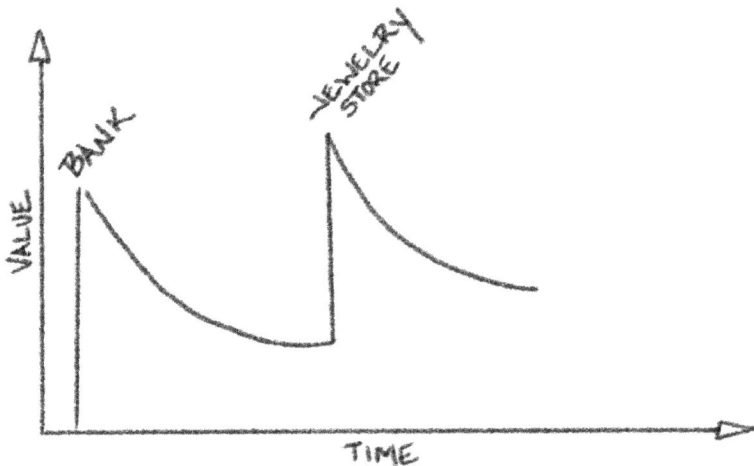

That is when the most recent owner bought the property. He bought it for a song at the bottom of its life, this time reinventing the buildings to house his business—a printing shop—back when offset presses and paper cuts were still a booming industry.

My notebook drawing was starting to look like an EKG for old buildings—spikes of reinvention, long fades of neglect.

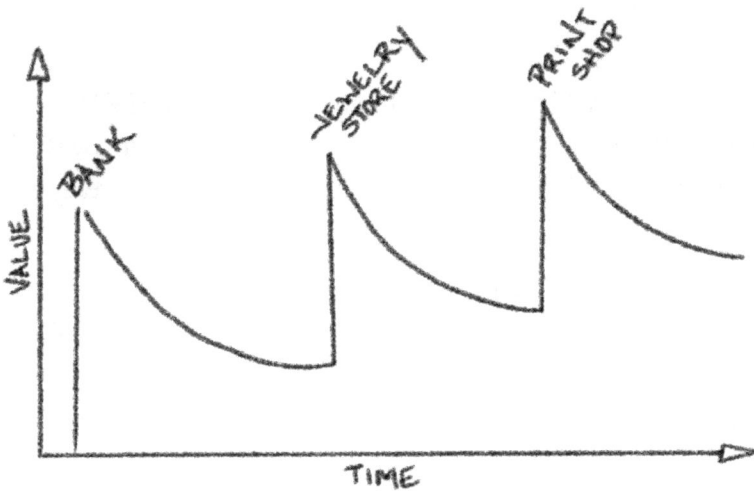

The business thrived for awhile, but eventually it too was shuttered as the old man aged. The space turned into little more than a personal storage unit until he passed away. It sat mostly untouched for decades, collecting dust and whatever else time decided to deposit.

Then came the 1980s. The corner building, in a bold leap of entrepreneurial spirit (and questionable zoning judgment), was converted into an X-rated movie house. That ran its course—until the city got wind of it and politely escorted the operation off the premises with a firm "no, thank you."

Vacant once again, the building became a venue for punk rock squatters in the '90s, who hosted underground concerts, did who-knows-what in the dark, and essentially treated it like a clubhouse for people who thought broken glass and discarded needles made great flooring. And somehow, through all of that, the electricity had stayed on. No one could say exactly why. Either the old man really believed in paying the power bill… or he just forgot to cancel it.

That was where we found them. Three buildings that had been sitting mostly empty for nearly twenty years.

They needed everything. Roofs, plumbing, electrical, HVAC, flooring—you name it, it had either rotted, rusted, or run away. The only thing that still looked like it had some life left in it were the 18-inch-thick brick exterior walls.

In other words: it was perfect. We could buy the property at a very low price because it had reached the end of its useful life. We were prepared to reinvent the space and invest a ton of money to bring it back up to a new highest and best use.

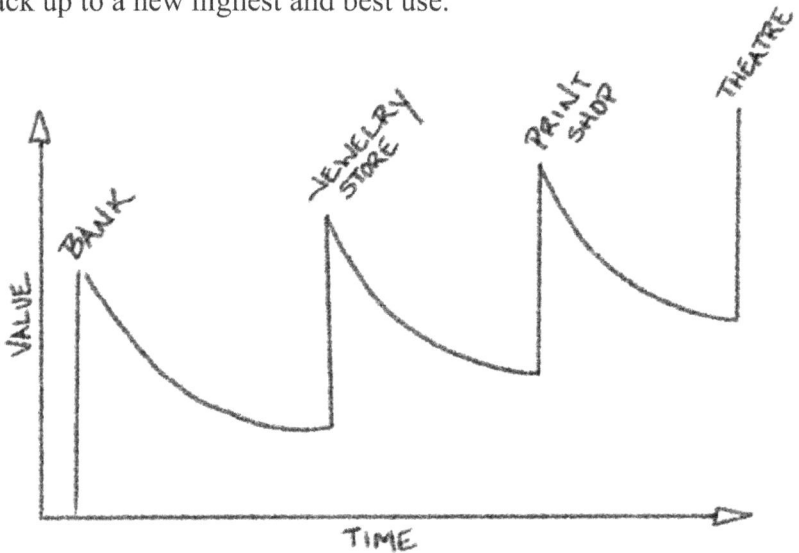

We'll take it!

I called the listing agent and started negotiations, which quickly felt less like a business transaction and more like refereeing a family feud.

The buildings were now owned by the old man's three adult sons—each one navigating life through a fog of addiction and mutual resentment. From the start, it was obvious they couldn't stand each other. They didn't want to renovate the buildings. They didn't want to split the proceeds. They just wanted fast cash and for the whole thing to disappear like a bad memory.

I played the part—walked them through how much work it was going to take to bring these buildings back to life. How they were in such disrepair that there was very little value to the buildings beyond just the value of the land.

I casually mentioned we were also looking at other properties downtown in better locations, where the floors weren't actively trying to eat you. Then I made what I thought was a low balled offer.

They didn't just say yes—they practically tackled it. I hadn't even finished the sentence when they were nodding, hands out, ready to sign. I stood there stunned. They had just agreed to sell three buildings for less than what other properties might rent for over the course of a year, just a few blocks away.

I didn't ask why. I didn't blink. I didn't even pause long enough to consider if they'd misheard me. It was clear they were grieving in their own ways. They wanted out and we offered them a clean exit.

We moved forward and prepared to buy the buildings.

Due Diligence – What are we Buying?

During the due diligence and escrow period, I spent a lot of time down at the buildings—walking the block, talking to neighbors, learning the rhythms of a place that had been asleep for decades. There was another old print shop still operating just down the street. The owner had been around long enough to remember when these buildings were alive with business… and then when they weren't.

He shared stories of the old owner, of how things used to be when presses clattered and people actually walked this part of downtown on purpose. But one detail stood out. He mentioned, almost offhand, that the previous owner had paid someone to put a new roof on the corner space not long before he passed. Apparently, the leaks had gotten so bad, something had to be done.

I perked up. That was no small detail. A new roof on one of the buildings? That alone could save us tens of thousands of dollars. It was the first glimmer of good news since we'd fallen through the floorboards on our first tour.

We hired an inspector, mostly out of formality. These were empty shells—we weren't expecting much beyond what we could already see: no mechanical systems, no finishes, no surprises. Still, we wanted to make sure there weren't any hidden time bombs behind the walls, under the floor, or above our heads.

That's when we got an even better surprise. Turns out, the roofing crew that had been hired didn't stop at the corner building. They replaced all three roofs—clean, sealed, and solid. That was amazing! How did the three sons not know about that? The roofs alone were worth nearly as much as we were paying for the entire building.

What started as a crumbling liability was now looking more and more like a diamond in the dust. The most expensive part of any renovation had already been taken care of… and we didn't even have to ask for it.

We closed on the buildings, and I got to work immediately. First up: demo.

50 Years of Pigeon Poop – The Return to a New High

As I mentioned, my wife was especially excited about this project. She was an actress, after all, and the idea of helping bring a new theatre to life—right in the heart of our town—lit her up. It wasn't just an investment anymore. It was personal. The arts had given her a stage. Now she was ready to help build one.

We suited up early on a Saturday morning, ready to tear into it. It was mid-spring, already warm, and even hotter inside the buildings. We showed up in shorts and t-shirts, donned with goggles, face masks, gloves, crowbars, and sledgehammers in hand. It was less "renovation crew" and more "DIY-themed episode of American Gladiators."

We started with the drop ceiling. Carefully, we placed 10-foot ladders across the gaps in the rotted-out floors, trying not to think too hard about how far we might fall if we missed a step. The excitement was palpable.

We were documenting everything—opening the door for the first time, crossing the threshold, pulling down the first water-stained tile. It was an Instagram photo shoot before Instagram even existed. Somewhere, there's a roll of film that captured two overly enthusiastic people covered in sweat and ceiling debris, smiling like they just won the lottery. That first day wasn't glamorous. But it felt like the beginning of something big.

I hooked a section of the drop ceiling with my four-foot crowbar and gave it a solid heave. Down came an avalanche of ceiling tiles, insulation, and fifty years' worth of sealed-in debris—all of it exploding into a choking dust cloud that made me instantly question every life choice I had ever made.

I couldn't breathe. I had to back down the ladder slowly, one rung at a time, just to find oxygen.

And then—I heard it.

Crunch.

As my steel-toed boot hit the floor, the unmistakable sound of breaking bones echoed through the space.

I froze.

There was no pain—so it wasn't me. My heart jumped. Was my wife okay? Had something fallen? Did part of the ceiling hit her? I looked down, blinking behind dust-coated goggles as the haze slowly began to clear.

That's when I saw it. Through the settling dust cloud, right at my feet, were the unmistakable remains of a small animal. Mummified. Crushed. Long dead—likely before we were even married. Based on the condition, it may have been the original tenant.

We needed air. Now.

Crunch.

Two of them? Huh?

Whatever those little guys were, they must've made their home up there decades ago—living their best life in the cozy darkness of a forgotten ceiling until time, gravity, and one overly enthusiastic renovation team brought it all crashing down.

Every step toward the exit was met with more of it—soft, brittle cracking underfoot like we were walking across a field of dry twigs. Except it wasn't twigs. It was bones and who knows what else.

We didn't stop to investigate. By the time we reached the front door, we were practically gasping for air. Fresh spring air hit us like a blessing. We stumbled out onto the sidewalk, coughing, wheezing, laughing in disbelief.

One look at each other, and we lost it. We looked like chimney sweeps who got in a fistfight with a coal furnace—and lost. Soot covered everything. Our hair, our clothes, our gloves, our skin. Even our eyelashes were grey. I wiped off my goggles, finally able to see clearly again. Took a breath that didn't taste like ceiling rot and cracked open a bottle of cold water. We'd been working for less than an hour.

When the dust finally settled, we cautiously peeked back inside. What we saw looked like a scene from a low-budget horror film— one where the villain wasn't a masked killer, but... birds.

That's when the realization hit. When the previous owner put the new roof on the building, he had sealed in an entire colony of pigeons. And judging by the sheer number of remains, that ceiling had been their home for decades. That wasn't just dust that had been falling on us.

It was fifty years' worth of pigeon poop.

I turned to my wife, who was already backing away like she'd seen enough for ten lifetimes. She didn't yell. She didn't freak out. She just gave me a look that said we are done here and made it crystal clear: someone else was finishing that demo. She told me she'd be back when the stage lights were being hung and the seats were bolted down—when it started to look like a theatre and not a crime scene.

Fair enough.

Rebuilding to the Highest and Best Use

I hired a few day laborers to finish the demo—guys with stronger stomachs and far less curiosity about what might fall from the ceiling. I was there every day, overseeing the work, managing the chaos, and slowly shaping the vision in my head into something real.

The project was exhilarating. I mapped out the floor plan, figured out where walls would go, where the lobby would begin and the stage would end. I was standing in the middle of what would become the dividing wall between the two spaces—one destined to be the lobby, the other, the theatre—when I heard a familiar voice behind me.

"Got a license for that thing?" he said, eyeing the sledgehammer in my hand like I was a child playing with explosives.

It was Yoda. He always had a way of showing up at just the right moment—half ghost, half building inspector, with a sixth sense for poorly-timed decisions. I grinned and handed him the hammer.

"No license," I said, "but I've got vision, a floor plan, and enough confidence to fake the rest."

He chuckled and took the sledge. "Let's put a dent in this dream of yours. You ready to bust this thing open?" he said, eyeing the brick wall like it had personally insulted him.

I nodded and handed him the sledge. "Been ready since the first pigeon carcass landed on my head."

The wall stood fourteen feet tall and eighteen inches thick— original brick, laid by hand. It had held up for over a century, but it was time. This would be the pass-through between the future lobby and the theatre space. Knocking it down felt like breaking through the past to make room for what was next.

We traded swings, brick by stubborn brick, sweat building up in the heat. Between the rhythm of the work and the occasional cursing at ancient mortar, my mind drifted back to the deal. About what had pulled me into this place to begin with.

The Path of Progress

He'd been around long enough to know how to read a street. And this one, rough as it still looked, had all the signs. Infrastructure was being upgraded. The streetlights a few blocks away were new. The city had quietly installed fresh utilities two blocks over. One of the big theatres down the street was getting a face lift. Restaurants were moving closer. The dust of revitalization was in the air. This wasn't luck. It was timing. Pattern recognition.

This property was squarely in middle of the path of progress. We weren't swinging hammers just to make a building look nice. We were putting our backs into a piece of the future.

He grabbed a carpenter's pencil and a brick we had knocked out of the wall and proceeded to recreate the napkin drawing he showed me a few weeks earlier when he was explaining the principle of the property life cycle. This time he added another line.

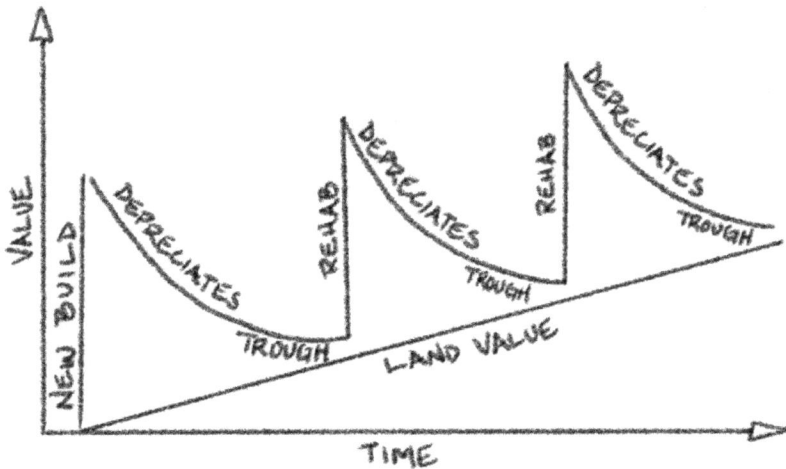

This line is the land value. When you have a property in the path of progress, the land value continues to increase over time. That's what we want to see in our investments.

The path of progress isn't about betting on what might happen someday. It's about seeing the early signs of movement and planting your flag in this path before the rest of the crowd shows up.

In a historic downtown, like this one, it moves like a tide creeping back in. It starts with a city grant to fix sidewalks. Then a café opens on the corner where a pawn shop used to be. Next thing you know, an art gallery displaying local artists moves in and suddenly parking is a problem again. Only this time for the right reasons.

That's where we were. Right in the middle of that momentum. This building wasn't just a theatre-to-be, it was a puzzle piece in a bigger picture. And that picture was starting to come into focus.

But the path doesn't just run through old neighborhoods. Out on the edges of the city, in the suburbs, it moves too—just with a different energy. There, it doesn't creep. It pushes.

You'll see it where big developers are cutting roads into farmland, where subdivisions follow new schools and widened highways like shadows. A new grocery store. A fire station. Then an entire retail corridor sprouts up in a spot where, just a year earlier, you couldn't get cell service.

Out there, the path of progress is drawn by bulldozers and concrete trucks. In town, it's revealed by investors and rehabbers. But in either case, the principle is the same: progress moves in predictable patterns. The key is to position yourself just ahead of it. Not so far out that you're guessing. And not so late that you're paying retail. The sweet spot is right in the turn—where it's not obvious yet, but it's no longer invisible.

That's what this deal was. That's why this building mattered. We knocked that wall down, one swing at a time, knowing full well it wasn't the first project, and wouldn't be the last. It was a solid confirmation that we were reading the signs right. The area was changing—slowly, quietly. But it was happening. And we had just bought three buildings smack in the middle of it.

The stage we were building inside? It wasn't just for performances. It was for a city block ready to return to life.

The P-cycle Revisited

From the moment it's finished—whether newly built or freshly renovated—it begins to age. Roofs wear out. HVAC systems fail. Paint fades. Tenants come and go. It doesn't matter how shiny it looks on day one—time gets to everything.

The key to successful investing isn't just buying low or selling high.

It's understanding where a property sits in its life cycle when you buy it—so you can plan accordingly.

Some properties are in their prime: stabilized, cash-flowing, with all major systems recently updated. Others are just hitting maturity—still functional, but needing strategic capital soon. And some... well, some are on life support. They're cheap for a reason. The price might look like a deal, but the property is whispering for help.

Too many investors don't know how to listen.

They walk into a worn-down property thinking they found a steal—something "undervalued." They throw on a fresh coat of paint, raise the rent fifty bucks, and pat themselves on the back.

Six months later, the roof starts leaking. The air conditioning system goes out. Suddenly, all that cash flow they were counting on is gone—and they're stuck in a money pit with a mortgage. The property wasn't a deal. It was a trap.

That's why knowing the P-cycle is critical. It's not just about the price. It's about the plan. If you're buying something at the end of its useful life, then you'd better have the budget, the time and the skills to bring it back to the beginning. And if you're not prepared for that, then what looks like opportunity can very quickly turn into liability.

This building we were standing in? It had already gone through its entire life cycle—more than once. It was physically tired. It wasn't just at the end of its life—it was already in the grave. But because we knew that, because we planned for it, we weren't surprised.

We knocked out the last brick. Sunlight slid from the lobby to the stage. The old place exhaled, and now had a place to land.

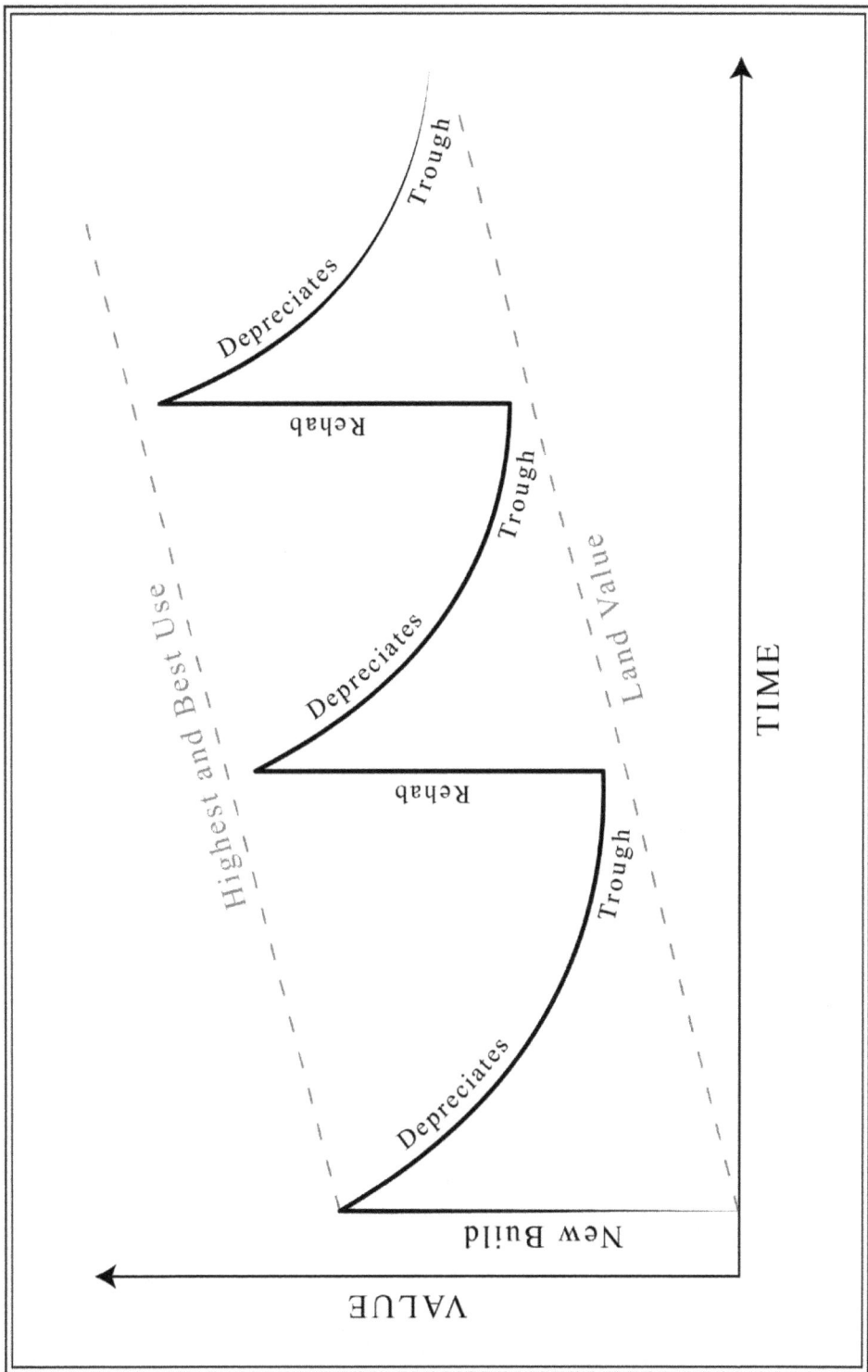

Depreciates

Trough

Rehab

Trough

Depreciates

Highest and Best Use

Land Value

Rehab

Trough

Depreciates

New Build

VALUE

TIME

Chapter Five

The Neighborhood Life Cycle

The 10,000 ft View: Neighborhoods cycle through phases; aligning the right property with the right Neighborhood phase, and your cash flow will soar.

It started with a noise in the kitchen.

Not a bang or a crash. More like… frantic tap-dancing on linoleum.

I had just cracked open the front door of a townhouse I was thinking about buying. The listing said "needs a little TLC," which we all know is code for: "Bring gloves and a flashlight. And maybe a priest."

On paper, it looked pretty good. Rents were strong in the area, especially based on the asking price. The bones looked decent from the photos. It was a two story brick townhouse in a small development of 18 units, located in Olde Towne.

I stepped inside and listened. Silence.

Then—*scritchscritchscritchSCURRYSCURRYSCURRY*—something tore across the floor just out of sight. By the time I cautiously edged around the corner and into the kitchen, whatever it was had vanished again.

More silence.

And then… chaos.

A blur of brown fur launched itself off the countertop like it was auditioning for the X-Games. I didn't even have time to think. Just pure survival instinct. I flinched hard, throwing my torso into a contortionist backbend that would've made a yoga instructor weep. It was full *Crouching Tiger, Hidden Squirrel*—arms flailing, knees bent, body mid-limbo like I was dodging a slow-motion uppercut from nature itself.

The squirrel flew over my shoulder in a blaze of panic and regret, banked a hard left mid-air like a tiny fighter jet, and bolted through the front door.

Gone.

I just stood there blinking, trying to process what had just happened.

Behind me, my real estate agent was wheezing with laughter.

"You good?" he asked between chuckles.

"Define good," I muttered.

We were standing in the living room of a freshly painted townhome. It looked like a great rental—two bedroom, two and a half bath, decent layout with double master suites, carpet that hadn't yet given up hope. It was solid brick structure. Everything looked good.

"I like it. Let's make an offer," I said.

The agent's voice got excited. "Great. And just so you know, the seller's got five more units in this townhome community that he is thinking of selling. If you're interested in a package deal, we might be able to work something out."

That's when the voice crept in—the one that whispers sweet nothings like *this is it. This is your opportunity. This was meant to be. This deal is special.* My mentor had warned me time and again: One deal at a time. More is not better.

But this was early in my career and it was a "once in a lifetime opportunity." It was too good to pass up.

Not to mention, this wasn't just a real estate deal; it was a declaration. Six brick townhomes out of eighteen in the development. That made me a one-third shareholder in this tiny kingdom. I wasn't just buying properties—I was buying an empire, a front-row seat to the multifamily dream I'd been sketching on napkins and underwriting in my sleep.

So I said yes. Bought all six. Didn't blink.

For a brief and glorious moment, I was king of the cul-de-sac. Strutting around like the real estate rock star I thought I was.

Things went pretty well at first. Rent checks coming in. No serious maintenance issues. And even though interest rates were still hanging out in the nosebleed section, the deal still cash flowed.

After I paid the mortgage, taxes, insurance, and tucked away a little reserve for life's inevitable curveballs, each property put about $100 in my pocket each month. That was progress.

Now, a hundred bucks didn't buy me freedom, but multiply it by six and it started to feel like traction. That was $600 a month—a week's pay back when I was still swinging a hammer and popping ibuprofen for breakfast. The numbers were tight, but they worked. I wasn't getting rich, but I was one step further down the path.

The Waterfall – Part 2

Years went by. I had scaled my business significantly, reached my breaking point on the beach in St. Thomas, and was now focusing on unwinding my portfolio with my mentor's guidance.

These townhomes became a focal point for one of his lessons.

With only a passing glance, focused just on the property itself, these units still appeared to be steadily humming along. Rents mostly still coming in, bills getting paid, and the properties quietly doing their job. But something was changing in the rhythm.

First, one of the tenants gave notice. They were leaving at the end of their lease. I didn't love it, but it was probably time to invest some money back into that unit. It was tired and going to need some work to get it ready again. It needed a full repaint, new carpet and the appliances were on their last leg. Oven degreaser alone definitely wasn't going to fly this time.

It was most likely going to chew through all of the cash flow I would earn over the entire year, and maybe part of the next one. Still, I wasn't rattled. This was part of the game. I had some reserves, a plan, and a good attitude.

The next month, the tenant moved out. I carved out a few days and headed over to start the turn.

It was a weekday morning. Commuters zipped by in button-downs drinking bitter coffee, chasing meetings and deadlines. I grinned. That wasn't me anymore. I wasn't clocking in to work on someone else's dream. I was working on my dreams today.

The feeling lasted right up until I cracked the door open.

This time it wasn't the scurrying sound of a squirrel caught mid-heist in the cabinets. No, this time the sound was softer… almost peaceful. Like a fountain.

Except there wasn't supposed to be a fountain.

I rushed in.

The living room greeted me with a gaping six-foot hole in the ceiling, water pouring through it like a waterfall. Two inches of standing water covered the floor. The subfloor had buckled and swollen into a shape that would've made a rollercoaster jealous.

Whatever dream I was working on that day—it had just become a nightmare.

I vaulted upstairs, two steps at a time, chasing the sound of rushing water.

No lights. Crap, I'd forgotten to get the power turned on.

So there I was, in a dark master bathroom, flashlight in hand, scanning for the source. Water was everywhere. The carpet squished beneath my feet with each forward step. The sound was unmistakable—full-force, like someone had cranked a garden hose to max and walked away.

Then I found it.

The toilet tank had somehow cracked clean across the back, right where it met the wall. The flush valve was still doing its job, trying to refill the tank as fast as the water could escape. Except it wasn't filling anything—it was draining straight through the subfloor and cascading into the living room below.

I dropped to my knees and grabbed the shut-off valve behind the toilet.

Locked up. Wouldn't budge.

I yanked and twisted, but it was frozen. Stuck in the open position—mocking me as the tank continued to drain into the floorboards.

I had been *here* before…and learned my lesson.

I bolted outside, heart racing, searching for the main shutoff like a man looking for oxygen. Started banging on neighbors' doors, hoping someone—anyone—knew where it was.

Nobody answered.

Of course they didn't. It was a weekday morning. Everyone was off at work, helping build someone else's dream.

Meanwhile, I was drowning in mine.

I finally spotted a cover near the curb, mostly swallowed by an oak root the size of my leg. It wasn't directly in front of my unit, but close enough. I pried the lid off, reached in, and shut the valve.

The water stopped.

So did the water to the rest of the building.

At that point, I didn't care. I needed the waterfall in my living room to stop.

I stood there catching my breath, not sure if I was soaked from sweat or the toilet shower I had just taken. I was half expecting my mentor to pull up behind me right at that moment with that look. The one that says, *"Is this the once in a lifetime opportunity you were looking for?"*

But this time, he didn't show. I was on my own for this lesson.

I grabbed a push broom from the truck and started sweeping water out the front door. It was a losing battle at first. The upstairs kept bleeding into the downstairs. It took hours for the floor to stop rippling under my boots.

Then came the carpet. I had to get it out of there.

As I peeled it back, the real problem surfaced. The subfloor wasn't plywood—it was particle board. What genius made that decision? That stuff had soaked up water like it was sponge on a mission, swelling until sections of the floor had buckled nearly four inches.

This wasn't a quick turn anymore. It was triage.

I cleared my calendar. No distractions. No side projects. Just this unit, this week. I needed it dried out fast—not just for the next tenant, but to keep mold from creeping in and setting up shop.

I ripped out every wet surface I could find, scrambled to get the power connected. I fired up dehumidifiers around the clock. The house hummed like a data center for days.

Then the AC went out. Seriously. How could this possibly be happening?

The Proposition

By the following week, I was knee-deep in construction. The old particle board was gone. I was back in my tool belt like the good old days, laying down fresh plywood—something that could actually hold its dignity if water ever paid another visit.

Midday, I stepped outside to grab another sheet from the truck. As I turned toward the sidewalk, I saw her.

Mid-thirties. Mini-skirt. Disheveled hair. T-shirt slashed at the collar and sleeves, hanging off her shoulder like she'd gotten dressed in a wind tunnel. She looked like someone had paused a Cyndi Lauper MTV video from 1985 and hit fast forward to today.

She stopped at the base of the stairs just as I stepped out.

"This unit for rent?" she asked, eyes darting up and down like she was scanning for a barcode.

"Yes," I said, switching into my best leasing agent voice. "Once the floors are in."

"How much is it?"

"Nine seventy-five," I replied.

Without missing a beat, she grabbed the hem of her skirt and hiked it a few inches. "How much for me?"

Toothless smile. Dead serious.

I froze. Brain empty.

"Twenty-five hundred," I blurted.

Wrong answer. Or maybe right. Hard to say.

She spun around and stormed off like I'd just insulted her negotiating skills. I wasn't laughing. Hard years were written all over her.

And right on cue, I heard it—the low rumble of my mentor's truck turning onto the street. Window down, elbow resting on the door.

"Who was that?" he asked.

You don't want to know. But he knew.

The neighborhood had changed.

The N-cycle

He climbed out of his truck surveying the scene. He had already heard about the dumpster fire I was cleaning up. And looking up and down the street the change was apparent. In both directions, you could see the overgrown yards, broken down cars and boarded up windows.

He bent down, grabbed a stick, and started sketching in the dirt.

"This," he said, pointing to the ground, "is the neighborhood life cycle. The N-cycle for short."

I watched as he waved his hand over the dirt. "Five phases. Every neighborhood moves through them. Some faster than others. Some get stuck. Some restart the cycle entirely. But all of them follow this rhythm."

He tapped the curve with the stick, then looked out across the street.

"With every investment," he said, "you've got to understand what phase the area is in. If you can learn to spot where a neighborhood is on this curve, you'll know exactly how—and when—to move."

He stood up and dusted off his hands.

Most investors don't fail from lack of effort. They fail from bad timing. They jump into a deal because it looks cheap and don't look at where the property is in the P-cycle, or the cycle of the neighborhood, the N-cycle.

He carried on, gesturing with the stick at the five distinct phases of the chart he had just drawn in the dirt.

Five Phases of the Neighborhood Life Cycle:

1. **Development** (New construction)

2. **Maturity** (Stabilization)

3. **Decline** (Physical Deterioration)

4. **Rejuvenation** (Major Rehab)

5. **Gentrification** (Major Rehab + New Use)

Phase One: Development

Development is the beginning of a neighborhood's life. Not just its first homes, but its first heartbeat. The roads are new. The sidewalks, still chalk-free. Street signs are crisp, fresh out of the ground. Parks are staked off. Schools are on the drawing board. It's the phase when nothing is finished—but everything is forming.

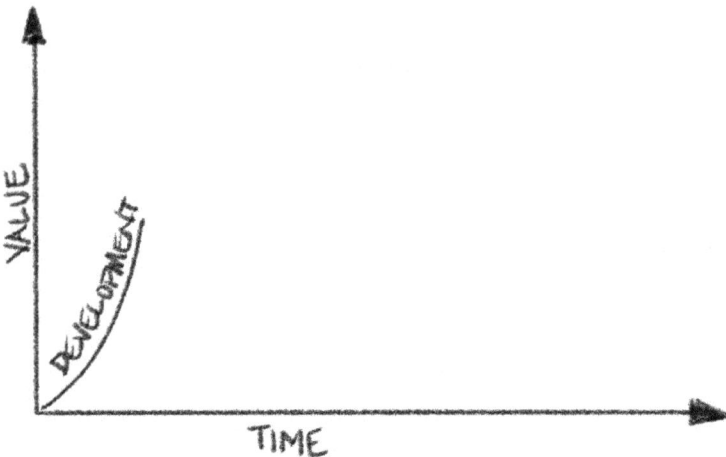

You can feel the momentum even if you can't see the finished picture.

Builders work in waves—grading dirt, pouring foundations, framing lots one section at a time. Whole streets emerge in a matter of months. Mailboxes multiply. Sod gets rolled out in long green carpets. And slowly, the idea of a neighborhood becomes real.

And as those homes rise, so do the prices.

Each new phase is released slightly higher than the last—just a few thousand dollars more per model. It's subtle at first, but it stacks up fast. The first buyers get in at base pricing. Then phase by phase, values climb—driven by scarcity, by momentum, and by the psychological pull of brand-new construction. Every foundation poured sends a signal: this place is growing.

Everyone moving in is new. Everyone's on the same timeline. Driveways fill with contractor vans and moving boxes. There's a sense of possibility—of shared beginnings. Families plant trees they hope will provide shade in twenty years. Kids race each other through empty cul-de-sacs. It's not just the houses that are growing—it's the roots.

And even though not everything is in place, you can see the bones.

The layout of the community. The traffic patterns. The future locations of schools and grocery stores. The builder has a blueprint, the city has one too—and in this phase, they're overlapping. Water lines go in. Fiber internet gets installed. New stoplights blink for traffic that hasn't arrived yet.

This is a phase filled with promise—and acceleration.

Phase Two: Maturity

Then the builders for-sale signs disappear and the construction noise fades. The only sounds now are sprinklers ticking across green lawns and the hum of an occasional lawn mower. Trees that once looked like twigs are now growing and have arched gracefully over driveways. Flower beds are established. This isn't a place being built—it's a place being lived in.

"This," my mentor said, "is what most people picture when they think of a stable community. Everything's in place. Nothing's in flux."

That's what defines the Maturity phase: stability. It's the sweet spot between growth and decline.

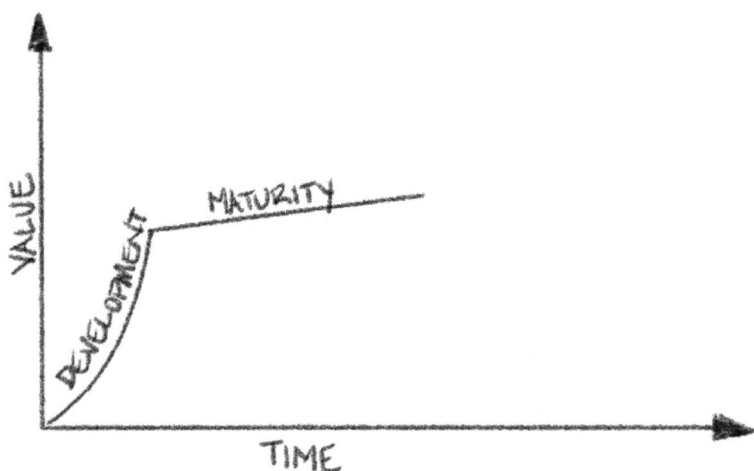

The builders are long gone. The model homes have been converted into real homes. Parks echo with laughter instead of hammering. At this point, the neighborhood has all its parts: schools, stores, stop signs, routines. People have history here. Driveways are full. Backyards are broken in. The rhythms of life have replaced the buzz of development.

Curb appeal is strong. Paint is fresh, but not factory new. Landscaping is thoughtful. Everything feels cared for. You'll see porch swings. Holiday lights done right. Neighborhood Facebook groups and block parties. The place has a personality now—shaped by the people who live there.

People buy here because they want peace of mind. Because they know what they're getting. The street names are familiar. The school ratings are established. The nearby shops and restaurants have loyal customers. Everything is predictable—and in real estate, that predictability is powerful.

In Maturity, the cycle flattens. Prices still rise, but much more slowly. The volatility is gone, and so is the outsized upside. What remains is stability. And for many homeowners, this is the dream: a safe, established neighborhood where the future looks a lot like the present.

But beneath the surface, time is still ticking.

Homes are aging. Not falling apart, but aging. Roofs creep toward the end of their lifespan. HVAC systems hum with a little more wear. Paint fades just a shade. And the capital reserves of many homeowners may not be keeping up.

Most people look at a mature neighborhood and see safety. And often, it is.

But timing matters.

Without consistent reinvestment, the cracks begin to show. First subtly: a sagging gutter here, a patchy lawn there. Then, more noticeably—a home that doesn't get repainted, a property that turns into a rental with less attention to detail. The charm is still there, but it's starting to slip.

If you buy a little too late into the cycle, just as that neighborhood begins to tip into fatigue, what looks like a safe asset can quietly become a liability. The paint dries. The edges wear. And slowly, sometimes imperceptibly, the picture begins to fade.

Phase Three: Decline

Here, the first clue isn't a broken window or a foreclosure sign.

It's a lawn.

Just one. Overgrown and wild, like someone has stopped caring. Then another. And then a mailbox leaning to one side, held up by a rope. The sidewalks, once chalked with hopscotch, now cracked and bare. It doesn't happen all at once. It never does. But if you pay attention, you can feel it: something has shifted.

"This," my mentor said quietly as he looked around the neighborhood where my townhouse sat, "is where most investors show up too late…or leave too early."

Decline is the third phase of the neighborhood life cycle. It's not a dramatic crash—it's a slow unraveling. A neighborhood that once brimmed with energy begins to lose its shine. The homes are still standing, the schools still open, but the pulse is weaker.

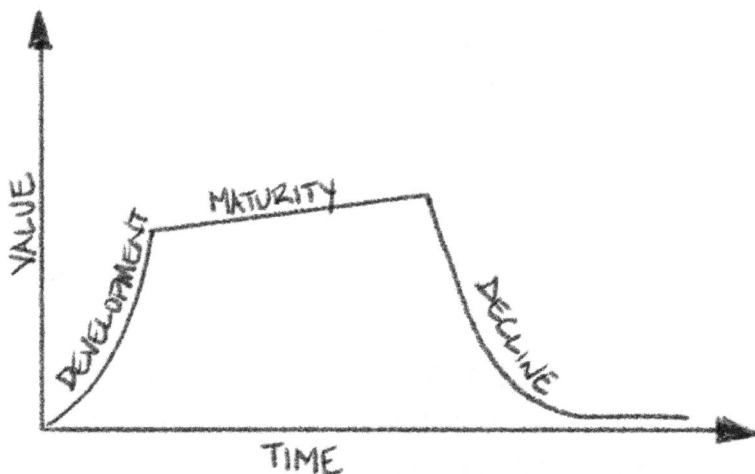

You start to notice deferred maintenance. Not everywhere, but enough to see a pattern. A missing shingle here. A car that hasn't moved in weeks. Paint that hasn't seen a brush in years. Small things, adding up.

Turnover increases. Long-time homeowners move out—sometimes aging out, sometimes cashing out. And they're replaced not by families putting down roots, but by landlords chasing cash flow. Rentals rise. Pride of ownership slips. And with it, the sense of community starts to thin.

Retail follows suit. The boutique coffee shop shutters. The chain restaurant goes dark. Vacant storefronts appear, and the "Coming Soon" signs stay up a little too long. Schools may lose funding. Local services start to lag. And slowly, demand dries up—not because people are fleeing, but because fewer people are choosing to stay.

The curve bends downward—then accelerates.

It's not always obvious from a spreadsheet. The prices look appealing. The rents might pencil out. On paper, the returns seem strong. But beneath the numbers is something much harder to quantify: a loss of confidence. A shrinking pool of buyers and tenants. A neighborhood slowly slipping out of favor.

Turnover increases. Long-time homeowners age out or move on. Rentals rise. Pride of ownership wanes. Retail anchors leave, replaced by temporary tenants—or nothing at all. Vacancy grows. Services lag. The bones of the community are still there, but the energy is gone.

The homes are aging, but unlike in Maturity, there's no reinvestment to catch the fall. Maintenance becomes too expensive or too delayed. Landlords patch instead of repair. Owners wait for a market upswing that doesn't come. And with each passing year, the gap between what the neighborhood once was—and what it could be—widens.

This is where many investors get caught. They mistake the discount for opportunity—without realizing that what they're actually seeing is a reduction in demand.

But Decline isn't the end of the story. It's a turning point. Because within this phase, two distinct forces can emerge—each capable of lifting a neighborhood into a new cycle of growth. One comes from within. The other from outside. And when either one takes hold, the neighborhood begins to change—again.

Phase Four: Rejuvenation

"Think for example about Brynwood." He said, referencing a well known neighborhood in our town.

It was a highly desirable neighborhood built in the 1950s—broad streets, tidy ranch homes, clipped hedges, and pride in every detail. At the time, it was one of the most desirable neighborhoods in the city. Good schools. Strong families. Block parties. A place where kids rode bikes until the streetlights came on and everyone knew whose dog belonged to whom.

But as time passed, the original owners aged in place. The homes aged with them. The shutters sagged. The flower beds faded. The optimism remained, but the energy didn't. By the 1980s, the charm had dulled. It wasn't neglected—it was just tired.

Then something beautiful happened.

The next generation started to arrive—not strangers, but often the sons and daughters of those original families. They had grown up riding those bikes and remembered the smell of fresh-cut grass in the summer and Halloween nights lit with porch lights and laughter. Now they were coming back—with young kids of their own.

They didn't just maintain the homes. They upgraded them. They knocked down walls. Opened up kitchens. Modernized bathrooms. Added square footage. They honored the bones of the homes, but took them to a whole new level. The schools were still great. The sense of community was still alive. And suddenly, the neighborhood that had gone quiet was buzzing again—with life, with laughter, and with rising values.

The curve steepened. Just like it had in the early days of Development. Except this time, the streets were already paved. The trees were already tall. This wasn't a new neighborhood—it was a renewed one.

That was the first Rejuvenation.

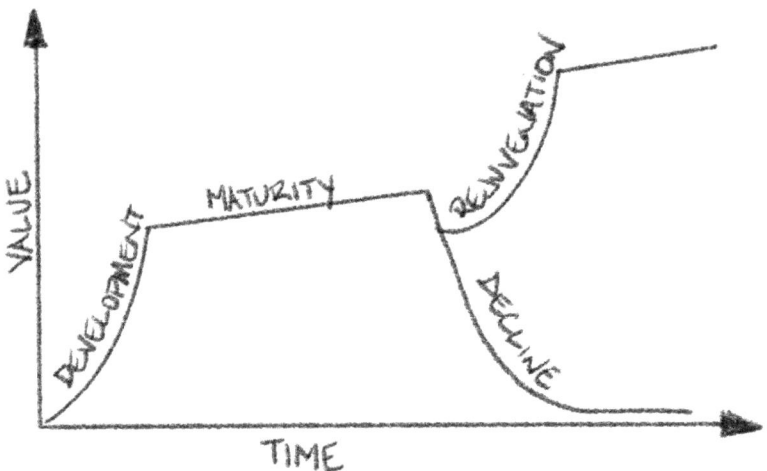

Eventually, as those families settled in and the improvements slowed, the neighborhood eased back into Maturity. The growth curve flattened again. The cycle doing what cycles do.

Then, in later decades—something remarkable happened again. Another wave reimagined the same bones.

And with that, the values soared—higher than they had ever been. Not because of speculation, but because of vision. Because people still believed in the neighborhood. Still saw it as a place worth investing in—not for a flip, but for a future.

That's Rejuvenation. And in the right neighborhoods, this phase doesn't happen once. It happens over and over again. One generation after the next. Like traditions passed down. When a neighborhood has good bones, good schools, and a good story— the reinvention happens organically.

One family at a time. One room at a time. One home at a time.

Rejuvenation doesn't chase progress. It nurtures legacy.

Phase Five: Gentrification

Where Rejuvenation begins early in the decline phase with families moving back into neighborhoods they've always loved, Gentrification begins late in the decline phase when people from the outside start paying attention.

It's not driven by nostalgia or a desire to return—it's driven by vision, capital, and proximity. Sometimes it's sparked by investor interest. Sometimes by city-led rezoning or development incentives. Sometimes, it's simply the pressure of geography—a neighborhood just too close to the city's core to stay overlooked forever.

You'll spot the signs. Empty lots start disappearing. A couple of restored homes near the edge of a historic district. A coffee shop that opens where a tattoo parlor used to be. An old brick building

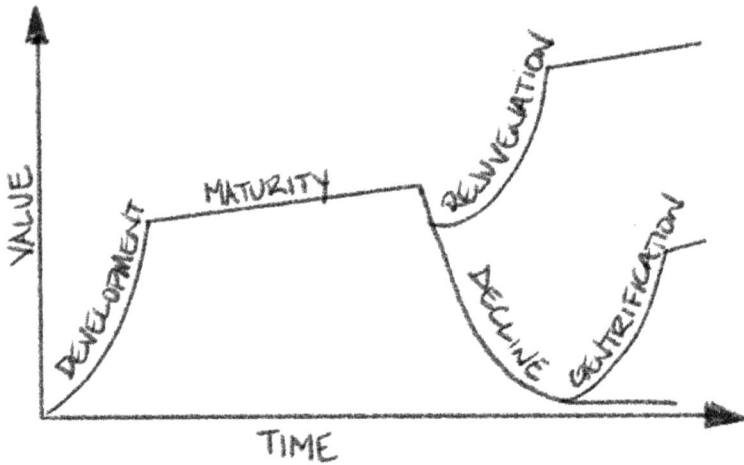

converted into a trendy wine bar with Edison bulbs and reclaimed wood. A yoga studio pops up down the block. Then a boutique bakery. Then a developer announces plans for a small mixed-use project on the corner.

Long-neglected buildings get swept up in coordinated renovation efforts. Streets once quiet with vacancy start buzzing with contractors and new arrivals. The neighborhood doesn't just change—it accelerates

The area is rebranded. Real estate agents invent new names for the neighborhood to make it feel fresh—names that have never appeared on a zoning map or tax record, but suddenly show up in listing descriptions. Prices rise. Then spike. The momentum feeds on itself.

This phase mirrors the energy and curve of Development: steep, fast, upward. Property values surge. Rent prices follow. The market moves quickly, and those who recognize the pattern early often realize tremendous gains.

But Gentrification is complicated.

Because it doesn't just rebuild—it redefines. The new version of the neighborhood may not feel like the old one. As new residents move in, old ones may be priced out. Longtime businesses shutter. Community ties stretch. The very soul of the place risks being rewritten in the pursuit of "improvement."

That's the paradox of Gentrification. It elevates—but it also displaces. It polishes—but often forgets what gave the place its shine in the first place.

Still, from a life cycle perspective, it's a natural stage of evolution. A response to scarcity. A product of market pressure. And in some neighborhoods—especially those close to urban cores with strong bones and good access—it's almost inevitable.

For investors, Gentrification offers opportunity—but it also demands responsibility. You're not just riding a wave. You're shaping the shoreline. That calls for more than market savvy. It calls for awareness. Respect. A willingness to build with—not just over.

Because eventually, the bulldozers leave. The scaffolding comes down. The excitement cools. And the neighborhood settles once again into Maturity—changed, yes, but cycling forward all the same.

The Line in the Dirt

There's a moment in every investor's journey where the lightbulb finally turns on—where all the reading, walking, driving, and spreadsheet crunching suddenly starts making sense. For me, one of those moments came standing on the sidewalk in front of that townhome looking at a chart drawn in the dirt.

It was time to sell this asset, and reposition into a different neighborhood. These deals were good deals when I bought them, but now we had entered the decline phase and there was no clear indication that the neighborhood would turn around anytime soon. There was a better location for me to hold my investments.

I grabbed my notebook and scribbled notes before the wind blew the chart away.

Neighborhoods don't move in lockstep. They meander. They stall. They skip phases, restart cycles, or evolve in ways no textbook can predict. Some hover at the edge of Maturity for decades. Others decline and never recover. And some, against all odds, rise again with renewed strength.

So the lesson isn't to treat the cycle as gospel. It's to treat it as a lens—a tool that sharpens your vision.

Once you understand what you're looking at, you stop evaluating properties in isolation. You stop getting distracted by finishes or price tags. And you start asking a better question: *"What phase is this neighborhood in—and is my strategy aligned with where it's going next?"*

You begin to see that a home in need of work isn't a liability if the streets around it are waking up. That a flawless renovation might underperform if it's in a place no one's moving toward.

You begin to move with intention. With patience. With the kind of confidence that only comes from seeing the bigger picture clearly.

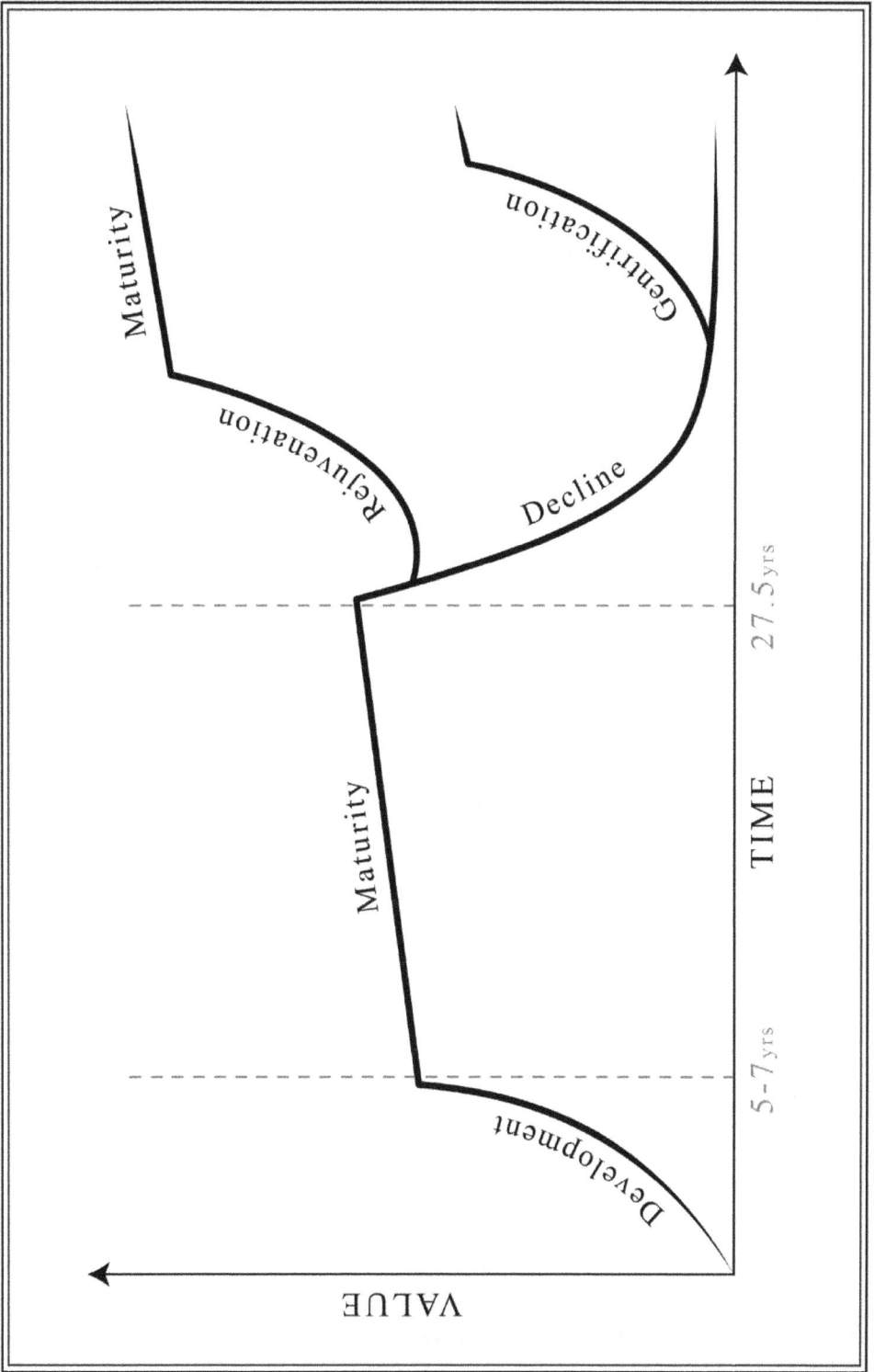

VALUE

TIME

5 – 7 yrs

27.5 yrs

Development

Maturity

Rejuvenation

Maturity

Decline

Gentrification

Chapter Six

The Market Cycle

The 30,000ft View:. Understanding the Market Cycle is like having a crystal ball in your tool belt, allowing you to see into the future of your investments with confidence.

"Do you think the market's going to crash?"

If I had a nickel for every time someone whispered that to me like they were asking if I knew the secret password to the speakeasy, I could probably buy another rental property—*cash*—with enough left over for a vending machine that dispenses anti-anxiety mints.

Sometimes it's that question. Other times it shows up in different costumes:
"Is now a good time to buy?"
"Did I miss the boat?"

Different phrasing, same nervous heartbeat.

What people are really asking is this: "What's about to happen—and how do I get rich...or also not get burned?"

And honestly, I don't blame them. The world of real estate advice is a mess. Like trying to get directions from your drunk uncle with no GPS and an opinion about everything. Cable news is screaming "DOOM". Some YouTuber is pacing in front of a chart that looks like a rocket launch countdown, swearing it's the market is about to take off—right after the sponsor break. And that guy at your gym? The one who thought "escrow" was a protein powder six months ago? Yeah, he's now confidently predicting interest rates.

It's a lot. And it's loud.

In the middle of all that noise, how are you supposed to think clearly and make smart decisions?

The answer lies in a singular tool my mentor shared with me early in my career, but I was too busy "scaling" to hear it. It was only after my teachable spirit returned, after my business nearly broke me and that existential gut punch on the beach in St. Thomas reset my thinking—only then was I finally ready to hear the lesson.

Markets Are Cyclical

We met at our usual spot—Countertop University—CTU.

The real estate market had completely melted down. Gone were the days where everyone was drunk on appreciation and easy money, where the cover of every magazine read: *"Real Estate Gold Rush"*. And everybody was buying real estate. When loan officers were handing out mortgages like Oprah handed out cars— *you get a house, you get a house, you get a house!*

Foreclosures were now at an all time high. Banks were trying to give properties away to any investor with a pulse that would take them, but there were very few investors left that were willing to play. Most of the "new" guys were sitting in the corner licking their wounds.

He didn't say much. He didn't have to. He already knew the question I was asking before I could even get it out. He just nodded, reached into his pocket, and pulled out a pen like he was about to sign a peace treaty between common sense and market mania. And then came the napkin.

"Everyone's a genius in an up market," he said, gesturing an upswing. "That's when it's fun. Until the tide goes out. Then we see who's really been swimming without their trunks on. The market isn't personal. It doesn't care how many deals you've done. It just cycles."

He looked at me the way only someone who's been through the wreckage can.

"You've been running hard," he said, his voice calm. "You've built something impressive. But now you're in a different phase of building your business. This isn't about adding more weight to the bar. It's about learning how to carry it without snapping your back."

He tapped the napkin, the ink of the drawing still fresh.

"You've got to stop reacting to the market," he said. "And start preparing for what's coming."

He didn't mean timing it like some Wall Street day trader with a caffeine addiction and three screens blinking in his basement. He meant understanding the rhythm of the market.

He slid the napkin toward me across the worn counter. Coffee-stained, edges curled, the ink starting to bleed into the paper fibers.

I looked down. Two arrows chasing each other in a circle—one labeled *Seller's Market*, the other *Buyer's Market*.

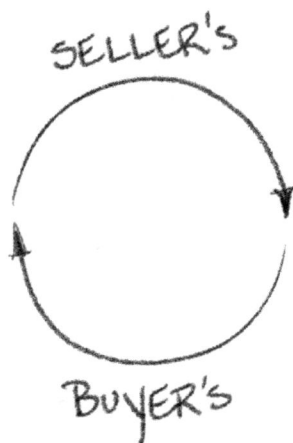

SELLER'S

BUYER'S

"You've heard of these, right?" he asked, already knowing the answer.

"Sure," I said. "Everyone has."

He nodded. "Yeah. And most folks think that's the whole story. The market goes up, the market comes down. Sellers on top, buyers on bottom, like some kind of economic teeter-totter."

He tapped the napkin with the end of his pen. "This is the part people *see*. The part that makes headlines. The part your barber has an opinion about."

I smirked. He wasn't wrong.

"Everyone's trying to guess where we are in the market. Buyers? Sellers? Is it over? Is it coming? They're watching the surface," he said. "But there is so much more going on in the ocean than just what you see on the surface."

Then he reached for a second napkin, and with a few quick strokes, stretched the circle into a wave—smooth, continuous, rolling from peak to valley.

"This," he said, "is what's really happening."

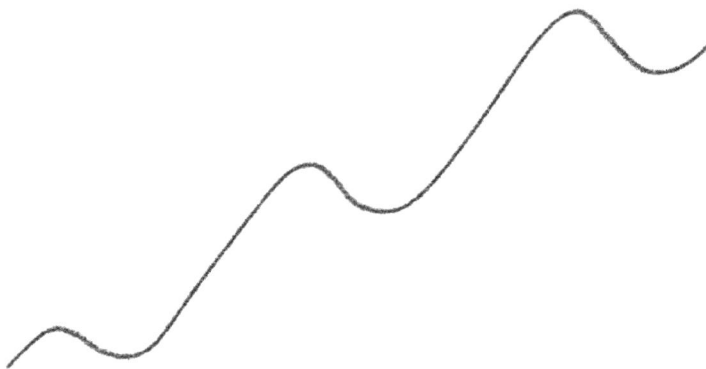

Time moving forward turns that circle into a wave. The market moves like the ocean. Swells. Crests. Crashes. Pulls back. Again and again. And if you can't see that wave forming… you're definitely the guy getting pummeled and tossed around the ocean floor.

I stared at the napkins.

Two crude drawings. And yet it felt like someone had handed me a crystal ball. A way to see into the future. He saw the look on my face—the squint of someone realizing they'd been sailing without a compass.

"The reality," he continued, "is that what you're looking at isn't just a flip between two moods. It's a cycle. A full one. With *four* phases. Not two."

> **Four Phases of the Market Cycle:**
>
> 1. **Seller's Market Phase I** (SM1 -Expansion)
>
> 2. **Seller's Market Phase II** (SM2 – Equilibrium)
>
> 3. **Buyer's Market Phase I** (BM1 – Contraction)
>
> 4. **Buyer's Market Phase II** (BM2 – Absorption)
>   aka *The Millionaire Maker Phase*

The Market Cycle

When a wave starts up out of the bottom of the trough, it is rising. Gaining momentum and picking up energy—that is the Expansion Phase (Sellers Market Phase 1 – SM1). This is when property prices are escalating, rents are growing and supply is dwindling.

It reaches full potential at the peak where the energy of the wave is at its maximum, and it enters the Equilibrium Phase (Sellers Market Phase 2 – SM2). The demand starts to wane as pricing hits all time highs. The market starts to slow.

Nearing shore and entering shallower water, the wave hits the bottom, dramatically slowing its energy and throwing the top over, breaking the wave. This is the Contraction Phase (Buyers Market Phase 1 – BM1). Now prices are falling, inventory is skyrocketing and real estate is becoming trash that no one wants.

Finally, the wave completes its cycle as the water pulls back. The ocean is reabsorbing the energy of the fallen wave, moving into the Absorption Phase (Buyers Market Phase 2 – BM2). Real estate values hit their lowest point here and the smart investors start to emerge. This is the most lucrative phase in the entire cycle for the smart investor. This is *the Millionaire Maker Phase.*

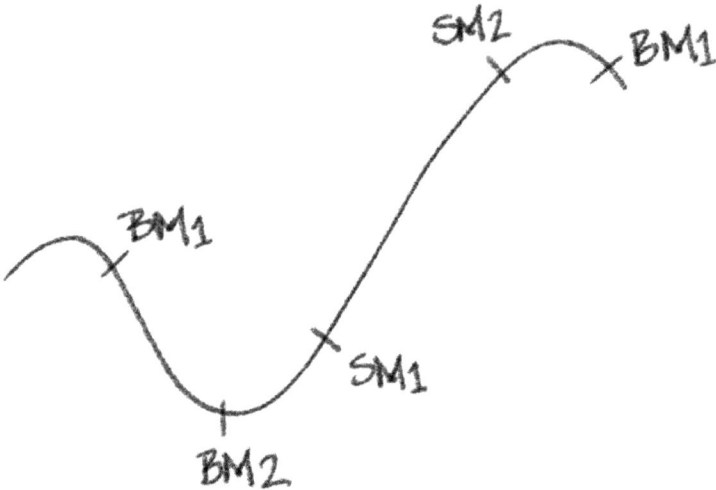

If you learn to spot these phases, you'll stop guessing about what is happening… and start knowing exactly what to do.

Reading the Waves

Standing there at Countertop University that day, coffee in hand and those two napkins between us, I didn't know just how right he was. Not then.

But looking back now, with the full weight of time and cycles behind me, I can say this with absolute certainty. He nailed it.

Exactly as he described. Each phase following the last one, moving in 3 to 5 year intervals, with the full cycle repeating every 12 to 18 years.

I obviously didn't absorb the whole lesson that day. There was no choir of angels or sudden enlightenment where I saw the entire ocean like I was Neo reading the Matrix. But one thing hit me right between the eyes with validation: Now was the time to make a move in my portfolio.

I didn't need perfect timing. I just needed to understand a shift was coming and start asking different questions.

Not *"Is the market going to crash?"* but *"What is the swell doing?"*

This was another important filter to continue the shift in my mindset from growth-at-all-costs to something more strategic. It wasn't about acquiring more properties—it was about positioning my portfolio to align with where the market was moving. Not where it had already been.

So, I started studying the patterns. Watching the cycle like it was the ocean. And as I looked more closely, one thing stood out: not all markets rise and fall the same way. Some cities danced to the tune of national headlines. Others moved to their own beat—slower, deeper, steadier.

By the time we hit the bottom of the cycle, I was prepared to move. I wasn't in a panic. I was ready to jump into action. I had clarity. I knew what my next move was.

Nationally, there hadn't been any meaningful new multifamily construction and development in decades. A trickle here and there, sure, but nothing substantial since the 80s. Meanwhile, renter demand had been climbing steadily, like kudzu on a pine tree, creeping up fast and no one was trimming it back. Homeownership rates were sliding. People were renting longer, later, or skipping ownership altogether—not because they had to, but because they *wanted* to.

We were entering what I started calling "Renter Nation."

At first, I saw it as a tailwind. More renters? More demand. Seemed like a win.

But then the second shoe dropped—and it wasn't a sneaker, it was a steel-toed boot.

If demand keeps rising, supply *always* follows. Capital chases opportunity. Big money would notice. Developers would notice. And they wouldn't build safe, modest apartments for working families. Oh no—they'd break out the champagne budget.

We're talking luxury. Ground-up builds. Rooftop pools. Fitness centers with more mirrors than weights. Dog parks with better landscaping than most public schools. Buildings so shiny they came preloaded with Instagram hashtags.

And that mattered. Partly because I didn't own those buildings. But mostly because I owned C-class apartment properties. Older apartments. Solid bones. Affordable rents. And I could see the writing on the wall.

The new A-class buildings would pull tenants up from B-class properties. And the B-class owners? They'd start sliding down the food chain, targeting *my* renters to backfill their losses. They'd slap on a coat of paint, throw in a washer-dryer, and call it an "urban upgrade."

Which left me, the guy holding the bottom rung, almost certainly facing a significant vacancy problem.

So I made a decision.

Partly from exhaustion and having built a business that was running me, and partly from reading the writing on the wall, I began preparing to exit my apartment portfolio. By reading the Market Cycle, I saw what was coming—and I'd finally learned how to listen.

Over the next few years, I sold off every apartment building I owned. One by one, I handed over the keys, nodded politely, and walked away like a guy leaving a party right before the cops showed up. This wasn't panic. It wasn't a fire sale. It was a clean, calculated shuffle toward the exit—done with the kind of calm that only comes from having a napkin map and a mentor who talked like he'd time-traveled through six recessions.

I wasn't hoping. I wasn't guessing. I was positioning—on purpose.

And wouldn't you know it? The Market Cycle showed up like clockwork.

The expansion took off again, and suddenly it was construction-palooza out there. Everywhere I looked, someone was laying a foundation, framing new builds like they were in a reality show called *America's Next Top Apartment*, and slapping the word "luxury" on anything with a gym and functioning plumbing. Developers multiplied like rabbits on Red Bull. Cranes dotted the skyline like acne on a teenage mall rat.

Then came the consequences.

Oversupply. Vacancy ticked up. Rent concessions came back like exes during the holidays—suddenly everyone wanted to give you something "just because." Free rent. Free deposits. Free toasters. I half expected someone to offer a free emotional support animal just to get a lease signed.

But by that time?

I was already gone. Shoes wiped. Page turned

While the rest of the market was adjusting their expectations and sweetening their incentives like over-apologetic waiters, I was somewhere else—quietly planning the next move.

With the apartment chapter closed, I had already gone back to the market cycle to look for new signals. Fresh footprints in the sand. Clues that something was about to shift again. I was open to any market in the country that would meet my investment targets.

Specifically, I was looking for job growth. And not just any job growth, I wanted *high-wage* job growth. Not "Now Hiring" signs flapping outside fast food joints. I was hunting for the kind of jobs that could lift a neighborhood's entire zip code. Jobs that came with health benefits, security clearances, and acronyms no one could pronounce. The kind of jobs that raise median incomes, and the number of Teslas in the school pickup line.

And that's when I saw it. Hiding in plain sight, right in my own backyard: Augusta, Georgia.

Now, Augusta isn't the kind of town that shows up on those "Top 10 Emerging Markets" lists next to photos of glass buildings and rooftop brunches. It's sleepy. It doesn't trend. It's more sweet tea than skinny latte. But I didn't need flash—I needed fundamentals.

And Augusta had them.

Specifically, Fort Gordon—a major military base tucked into the city like a secret weapon. Word was, the U.S. Army Cyber Command was gearing up for a massive consolidation. All their scattered cyber operations? They were going to put them under one roof. One location. One fortress of digital doom-prevention.

And Fort Gordon? It had the infrastructure. It had the location. It had the momentum. And best of all, nobody was talking about it—yet.

While the headlines were still fawning over Austin and chasing unicorns in Silicon Valley, I saw Augusta quietly stretching its legs like a sleeper cell of economic potential.

So I made my move.

When the military made the official announcement, I was already in motion. While the rest of the market was still Googling "What is Cyber Command?", I was lacing up my boots and writing offers. I didn't need to react—I was already in position. Like a guy showing up to a surprise party he helped plan.

I went heavy into single-family rentals in Augusta. Precision buying. One clean deal at a time. I wasn't swinging wildly. I was picking my shots like a sniper with a real estate license. My target, high quality homes in the best school districts.

And the results? Absolutely ridiculous over the next market upswing.

Rents jumped by an order of magnitude. Home prices nearly doubled. Cash flow soared like it had been shot out of a T-shirt cannon at a financial independence rally. Properties appreciated faster than a rocket-powered elevator with no brake button. Every metric moved in the right direction—and then some.

It became one of the most profitable runs of my entire investing career. But even then, even at the height of it, I didn't let the wave fool me. Because if there's one thing I'd learned from the cycle, it's this: good times don't last forever. Not in markets. Not in Mardi Gras. Not even in Augusta.

By the time we hit the next peak, I was prepared. Inflation surged like it had chugged three energy drinks and a bad idea. The Fed started cranking interest rates like they were trying to cool down a jalapeño economy with a fire hose. Demand softened. Bidding wars evaporated. And just like that—*snap*—the market shifted again.

And wouldn't you know it? The questions came flooding back like they were in a group text:

"Are we headed for a crash?"
"Is this another 2008?"
"Is it over?"

Same fear, different headlines. It was like déjà vu with a higher mortgage payment.

People were bracing for impact like they'd seen a crash coming from their Ring doorbell camera. Cable news dusted off the doom fonts. Finance influencers rebooted their recession thumbnails. And suddenly, everyone from baristas to barbers were offering their hot take on monetary policy—as if Jerome Powell had been calling them directly.

I remember that day like it was yesterday. My mentor pointing at me with his pen, saying, "People love to call the market a sea monster—wild, unpredictable, half-mythological. But it's not.

If you watch it long enough, it'll tell you what it's about to do. You just have to know the signs."

See, the wave doesn't just *happen*, it builds. Sometimes it whispers. Sometimes it clears its throat and gives you a full-blown sermon. Most people don't even notice.

The Seven Forces that Shape the Swell

Over the years since that first Market Cycle lesson at CTU, I came to understand there are invisible forces—seven of them to be precise—that shape everything. The patterns that build the swell before it breaks. While most rookies are standing on the beach, staring at the horizon like it owes them an explanation, the pro surfers—the smart investors—they're scanning for signs.

Seven Key Indicators of the Market Cycle:

1. **Inventory**

2. **Pricing**

3. **Time on the Market**

4. **Employment**

5. **Investor Activity**

6. **New Construction Activity**

7. **Foreclosures**

---

1. Inventory – The Tide

Inventory is the tide of the market.

When inventory rises, it's like the tide coming in. The water gets deeper. More homes are for sale. Supply is growing. And with more water beneath you, the conditions shift—waves can grow faster and break harder.

When inventory falls, the tide pulls back. The water gets shallow. Listings dry up. Supply tightens. And waves lose steam before they reach the shore.

Inventory doesn't create the wave—but it absolutely shapes its power. Rising tides build pressure. Falling tides expose opportunity.

2. Time on Market – The Frequency

Time on market is the rhythm of the ocean.

When homes are selling fast, the waves are coming in tight sets—closer together, higher energy. The market is moving. Buyers are paddling hard to catch what they can. There's urgency in the water.

When listings linger, the sets spread out. The frequency slows. The lineup gets quiet. Fewer buyers are paddling. The market is hesitant. Still. Waiting.

Time on market doesn't change the size of the wave—but it tells you whether the pulse is building… or fading.

3. Pricing – The Amplification

Pricing tells you how big the waves are, and how intense the ride might get.

When the market builds momentum, pricing is the amplifier. It magnifies the crest. What starts as a gentle swell suddenly towers overhead. Each sale pushes the next one higher. Confidence grows. Frenzy builds. Buyers stretch. Sellers smile. The wave gets bigger.

But when the cycle turns and the energy fades, pricing doesn't just deflate the swell—it deepens the trough. It exaggerates the dip. Discount signs go up. Reductions multiply. Sellers chase the market down, and the wave that once carried you now threatens to pull you under.

Pricing reveals the amplitude of the wave—the market. It shows you not just direction, but force. How strong the movement is. How fast it's accelerating. And how much power is packed inside the next set rolling your way.

4. Employment – The Current

Employment is the current that drives the waves before they ever hit the shore.

Long before prices climb, before inventory tightens, before buyers line up around the block—job growth starts moving. It's the underwater force that shifts the entire ocean. Strong, steady employment (especially high-wage jobs) builds pressure beneath the surface. It draws in people, raises incomes, boosts confidence. That current lifts the wave giving it energy from underneath, pushing the market toward expansion.

But when layoffs hit, or hiring freezes set in, that current turns. The water slows. Forward motion fades. Even if everything above the surface still looks fine—homes listed, prices holding—the wave is already losing steam.

That's why smart investors watch the current. They track who's hiring, who's leaving, and where the paychecks are headed. Because when the current shifts, a new wave is forming. And when it stalls, it's a sign the ride might be over.

Employment won't always make a splash—but it's the current that makes the market move.

5. Investment Property Activity – The Surfers

Out in the lineup, the best signal isn't the wave itself—it's the surfers. When the seasoned surfers start paddling into position, quiet and early, you know the swell is coming. They're not guessing—they're reading the water. They've seen enough cycles to know when to move and when to sit.

But then come the rookies – the kooks.

Late to the party, loud as a Bluetooth speaker, and convinced they're pros after one YouTube video. They crowd the break, jostling for position, stealing waves, falling off boards, crashing into each other. It's not strategy—it's FOMO in a wetsuit.

And when that happens? The seasoned surfers start paddling back in, calmly and quietly—before the chaos wipes out the whole lineup.

Investment property activity is the same. When experienced investors are entering early, it's a sign the wave is building. When the crowd piles in late, it's a sign the peak is near. And when the lineup suddenly clears? Something just shifted beneath the surface.

Watch the other surfers. The smart ones always move first.

6. New Construction – The Beach Crew

Builders are like the early morning crew at the shoreline—out before the sun, raking up seaweed, dragging driftwood out of the surf zone, setting out beach chairs and umbrellas. Not because the crowd is already here, but because they know it's coming.

They're not chasing the waves—they're preparing for them.

When new construction activity ramps up, it means the pros see a swell building. Maybe it hasn't hit the beach yet, but the signs are there: job growth is stirring, prices are climbing, inventory is thinning. And those builders? They're getting the shoreline ready. Homes start going up. Roads get paved. Signs appear with catchy names like "Sunset Pointe" or "The Preserve at Willow Creek."

But when they stop—when construction halts mid-frame or the model home goes dark—that's not just a pause. That's a warning. It means the swell has stalled. Maybe the current shifted. Maybe the last wave knocked too many people off their boards. Whatever it is, the beach crew has called it: today's not the day.

That's why watching new construction is such a reliable indicator. It's not about what's happening now. It's about what the builders believe is coming next.

7. Foreclosures – The Storm Surge

If employment is the current and inventory is the tide, then foreclosures are the storm surge—the sudden and violent flood that comes when economic weather turns ugly.

They're not subtle. When foreclosures rise, it means the market's foundation has cracked. Prices have fallen. Jobs have vanished. Homeowners are underwater—literally and financially—and the market is coughing up what it can't hold. It's chaos. The surf isn't clean—it's churned and dangerous.

The seasoned surfer knows: the best sets don't come in the middle of the storm. They come just before—when the energy is building and the swell is crisp and powerful. That's when the smart ones have already made their moves and are out past the break, riding the last clean waves before the surge hits.

By the time the storm crashes through and the lineup turns into a washing machine of debris and foam, they're already out of the water—dry, watching.

What follows the storm is messy. Loud. Unruly. But give it time. The ocean calms. The noise fades. And that's when the next clean sets begin to form. Quiet. Perfect. Ready for those who never stopped watching.

Foreclosures tell you when the market breaks.

The Market Cycle & Key Indicator Dashboard

Indicator	SM1 Expansion	SM2 Equilibrium	BM1 Contraction	BM2 Absorption
1. Inventory	↓ Falling	↑ Slowly Increasing	↑ Aggressively Increasing	= Flattening
2. Time on Market	↓ Falling	↑ Increasing	↑ Aggressively Increasing	↓ Falling
3. Pricing	↑ Rapid / Overheated	= Flattening	↓ Correcting	↑ Increasing
4. Employment	↑ Strong	↓ Weak / Declining	↓ Slowing / Unstable	↑ Gradually Increasing
5. Investor Activity	↑ Increasing to a Peak	= Flat	↓ Aggressive Pull Back	↑ Increasing
6. New Construction	↑ Aggressive Growth	↓ Declining	↓ Paused / Limited	↑ Ramping Up
7. Foreclosures	= Minimal	= Minimal	↑ Spiking	↓ Falling

Ride the Wave

He slid the last napkin across the counter, ink-smudged and coffee-ringed, then leaned back like a surfer watching the horizon between sets. We'd been at it for hours—talking cycles, signals, strategy—while the world outside kept spinning. But inside CTU? The noise had quieted. The fog had lifted.

He tapped the sketched-out wave. "This," he said, "is how you thrive out there. Not by chasing the perfect wave. But by learning when the next one is coming."

I nodded. Slower this time. I was finally starting to see it. The rhythm. The pattern. The swell.

Most investors? They're out there paddling like maniacs, trying to drop in at the exact peak—hoping to sell high, buy low, and retire somewhere with a drink shaped like a pineapple. But that's not strategy. That's gambling with better lighting.

He closed the folder with a soft *thud*, like a well-waxed board being set down on sand.

"That chart?" he said, patting it like it had taught him everything. "It's not just theory. It's tide, timing, and tempo. Once you understand the cycle, you stop flinching every time the headlines yell 'Crash!' or 'Boom!' You don't need to guess anymore."

He drained the last of his coffee, now more silt than sip, and gave me a nod.

"You stop fearing the ocean," he said. "You start riding the waves."

So now, when people ask, *"Is the market going to crash?"*

I ask them: *Are you ready for the next wave?*

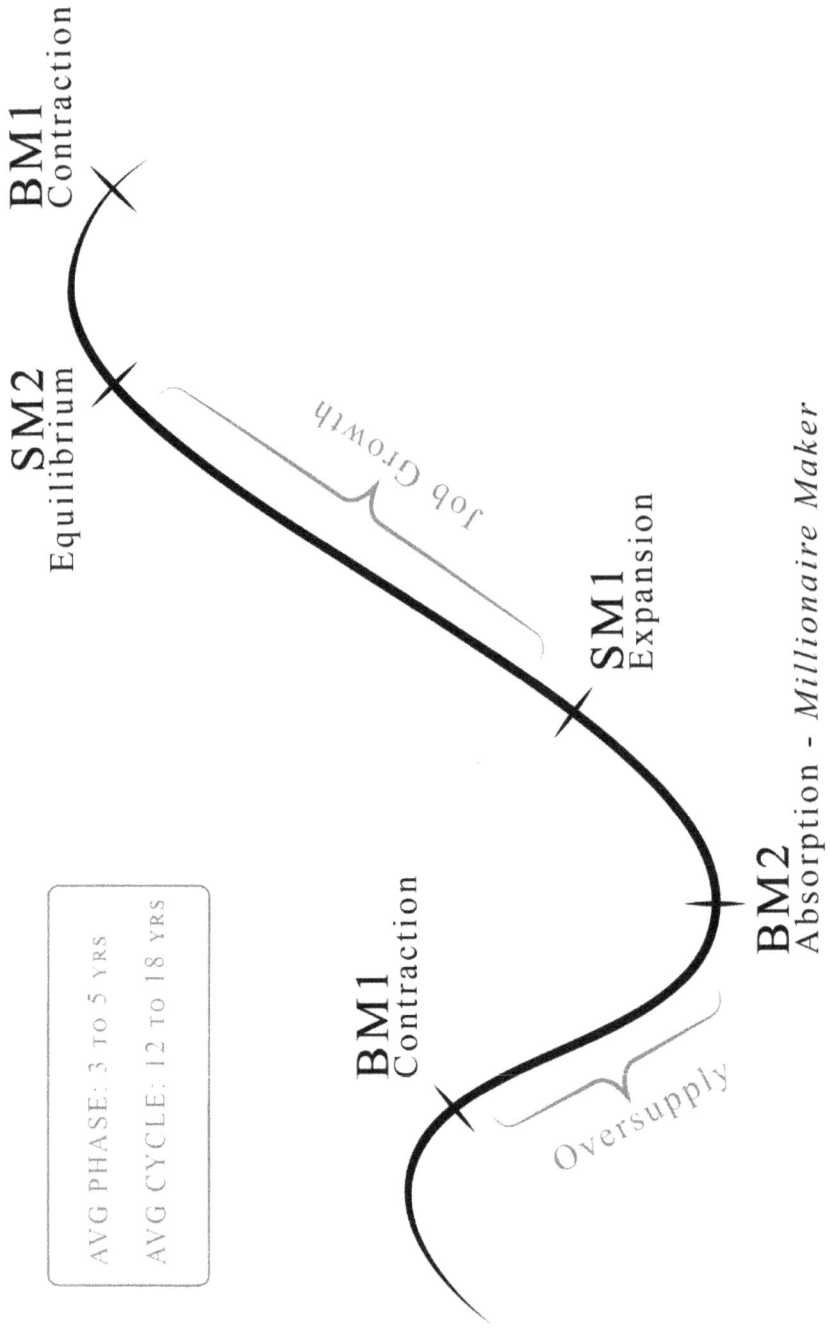

BM1
Contraction

SM2
Equilibrium

Job Growth

SM1
Expansion

BM2
Absorption - *Millionaire Maker*

BM1
Contraction

Oversupply

AVG PHASE: 3 TO 5 YRS

AVG CYCLE: 12 TO 18 YRS

Part III
Why Real Estate?

Chapter Seven

Price vs Value

You can ride every market wave perfectly and still wipe out if you don't know the difference between what's cheap... and what's truly valuable.

The Price Trap

The morning sun was just starting to burn off the mist as we rolled down a quiet stretch of cracked asphalt. It was early in my career. I was following my mentor's guidance and looking at a lot of rocks.

I sat in the passenger seat of his old red Chevy—window down, elbow out, half-listening to the soft hum of the tires while I thumbed through fresh listings on my phone.

He was quiet, like usual. Hands loose on the wheel. Watching the road. Watching the neighborhoods.

We were supposed to be scouting investment areas—driving blocks, feeling the rhythm of a few pockets that had shown promise—but my head was somewhere else. I'd spent the whole morning devouring stale MLS listings, backlogged off-market properties, and price drops that smelled like desperation. I wasn't looking for beautiful. I was looking for cheap. Under-market. Undervalued. Anything I could scoop up, slap some lipstick on, and convince myself the cashflow looked good.

"I think I found one," I said, more to my screen than to him. "Duplex. Southeast side. Seller's old, needs out. I can probably get it for five under ask. The spread looks good on paper if—"

That's when he turned.

Not toward the duplex. Not even in the right direction.

We veered off the main road and pulled into a tired strip mall with sun-bleached signage and a pothole parking lot. A nail salon. An empty café. And a liquor store that hadn't been open in a while. He slowed to a stop in front of a pawn shop.

"What are we doing?" I asked, half-laughing, half-annoyed.

"Need to show you something," he said, killing the engine and swinging the door open.

"Seriously? This place?" I glanced around. "Come on, we've got deals to chase."

He smirked—the kind of smirk that usually meant I was about to learn something, whether I liked it or not. "Trust me. This is a deal."

Inside, the air smelled like dust and decades of old smoke. The hum of flickering fluorescent lights buzzed overhead. Guitars with frayed strings hung on the walls. Shelves overflowed with tools, electronics, and half-forgotten junk. It was the kind of place where memories came to be bartered and boxed.

"This place is a graveyard," I muttered, trailing behind him.

He didn't respond. Just walked over to a glass case near the front of the shop and pointed at a small, unremarkable watch sitting alone on a velvet tray.

"Take a look," he said.

I leaned over. Brown leather strap. Simple face. Clean lines. A little faded. The tag read $450.

"Okay...?"

"That's a vintage Omega Seamaster," he said. "1950s. Maybe early '60s. In good condition, it might sell for five grand. Maybe six."

Now he had my attention.

"So... this is a deal?" I asked, tilting my head like a dog hearing jazz for the first time.

He shook his head. "Not really."

He motioned for me to lean closer. "Look at the crystal, it's scratched. The crown's aftermarket. The band's not original. No box, no papers, no service history. No provenance. Just a watch... with a story you can't verify."

Then he hit me with the line that split my thinking right down the middle.

"Price is what someone's asking. Value is what it's actually worth."

I stared down at the watch again, suddenly aware of how little I'd really seen the first time I looked.

He continued: "Price is a surface number. It's based on urgency, emotion, guesswork, and sometimes desperation. But value—that's deeper. Value is based on quality. Driven by things like demand and scarcity."

I nodded slowly, trying to keep up, but he could see I hadn't really gotten it yet.

"You're out there chasing price tags," he said, now turning toward me. "Trying to scoop up whatever's cheap. Thinking you can sprinkle some magic dust on it and turn it into gold. But price alone won't tell you what you're actually buying. Cheap can cost more than you think."

He tapped the glass.

"This isn't a deal. It's just less expensive than something else. And that's not the same thing as being valuable."

I felt it—a tectonic plate inside my investor brain creaked and moved.

As we climbed back into the truck and pulled back onto the road, I found myself staring out the window, but I wasn't thinking about deals anymore. I was thinking about everything I *hadn't* been seeing. The missing paperwork. The scratched crystal. The worn leather. The story behind the watch that no longer had a voice. And then I thought about all the properties I'd been rushing to see lately, so focused on the discount that I never stopped to ask what the real worth was. What they would give me... or cost me... over time.

A few blocks later, I turned to my mentor.

"Alright," I said, flipping to a clean page in my notebook. "If price is just what someone's asking, and value is something deeper, then how do you actually know when something's valuable?"

He gave me a quick side glance, half proud, half amused. He eased the truck down a side street lined with old oaks and tidy porches.

"You're asking the right question now," he said, turning the wheel into a quiet neighborhood. "That's the question that separates investors from speculators."

What Makes Something Valuable

The truck rolled through the neighborhood in a slow rhythm, the hum of the tires and the occasional blinker filling the quiet. I sat still, one elbow resting against the door, notebook slack in my lap. We weren't talking, but it wasn't the kind of silence that asked to be filled. It was the kind that settles in when you're chewing on something you can't quite let go of.

That watch had stirred something.

I looked over at my mentor. He was focused on the road, but I could tell he was waiting. Waiting for me to catch up. Not to him, but to the next question I needed to ask.

I flipped to a clean page in my notebook and finally broke the silence. "So, how do you know when something's actually valuable?"

He didn't look over, just nodded like he'd been expecting that. "Now you're starting to think like an investor," he said as he smiled.

The neighborhood he had turned into looked like it had been plucked out of a Norman Rockwell painting. The kind of place where porch swings were still used in the evenings and lawns told stories about who lived inside. He slowed the truck to a crawl under the big arching oak trees, scanning both sides of the street with a practiced eye. Not searching, exactly, but observing. Reading.

"There are four things I look for," he said finally, his voice even. "Four filters I screen all my deals through to determine if it's valuable enough to buy."

I clicked my pen and leaned in. I could already tell, he was about to reveal the smart investor decoder ring.

He held up a finger. "Number one: Cash Flow."

He let the word settle before continuing. "Does it cash flow? Simple as that. After you pay the mortgage, cover the taxes and insurance, set aside for maintenance and reserves—what's left? If it puts money in your pocket every month, it's creating value."

He tapped the steering wheel with a slow rhythm, his eyes still scanning the street like the homes themselves were nodding in agreement.

"You don't need a calculator to understand it," he said. "If your income is higher than your expenses, you've got a machine that's working. Not a firework show. A slow, dependable, boring-as-oatmeal money machine. And boring," he added, "is beautiful."

He glanced at me as if to check whether the cement was setting. "When rents rise over time, which they usually do, and your costs stay fixed, that machine you built starts to pay you more and more. It's not just value today. It's growing value. That's what makes it powerful."

I wrote "*Cash Flow = Value*" in my notebook.

He raised a second finger. "Number two: Scarcity."

He was talking about supply. How many homes like the one you are thinking of buying are even for rent in the neighborhood right now? How many are move-in ready? How many check the boxes most tenants are looking for?

He glanced over at me. "The fewer there are, the more control you have. Especially when demand holds steady. Scarcity doesn't mean 'special.' It means 'limited' in the places where people actually want to live."

The neighborhood had maybe 400 homes total. At any given time, maybe two or three came up for rent. If mine was one of them— and it looked good, was priced right—people would notice. It would rent quickly.

That made perfect sense. It wasn't about what a house had. It was about how few others had it.

I scribbled a word beneath "Cash Flow" in my notebook.

Scarcity.

He raised a third finger. "Demand."

"Have you ever tried to rent a house in a market where people are desperate to live? I mean the neighborhoods where people are lining up to get in." He asked. "Phones ringing off the hook, applications rolling in before the showing, tenants offering above asking just to lock something down?"

"That," he said, "is demand." tapping the wheel with his knuckles.

It's not about what the market *says*. It's about what people *do*. It's behavior. Urgency. Competition. When people want in, they don't wait. They move. They compromise. They overpay.

We turned down another street in the neighborhood. A delivery truck idled at the curb. A kid zipped by on a scooter. Lawns were neat. Cars were parked straight. The neighborhood had a pulse. An energy you couldn't quite quantify but couldn't miss either.

He motioned toward the houses around us. "This isn't Beverly Hills. But try getting a rental here in July. You'll have ten families calling before the listing even hits Zillow. That's demand."

I scribbled a note: Demand shows up in behavior. Not just data.

Neighborhoods with real demand don't just attract people. They retain them. People plant roots. They tell their friends. They bring their families. When that happens, your vacancy stays low. Your rents stay strong. Your asset grows in value, without you chasing the numbers.

I looked back at my notebook.

Cash Flow. Scarcity. Demand.

He held up a final finger. "Longevity."

We slowed in front of a brick ranch—three bedrooms, two baths, neatly kept. The kind of house most people might scroll past in a listing because it didn't scream anything loud. But it was clean, functional and updated.

He nodded toward it. "This one? It's got longevity."

He let the truck idle in the street as he started pointing things out.

Open layout. No need to tear down walls to make it livable. Bedrooms are good-sized. Primary suite has its own bath. Kitchen's been updated, but it's not trendy, just clean with timeless finishes. Brick exterior means low maintenance. Roofline is simple. HVAC's newer. It's move-in ready now, and it'll still make sense twenty years from now.

And when you put money into it? You use quality materials. Not builder-grade particle board that swells if someone says 'humidity' too loud. I'm talking durable, well-installed upgrades—stuff that *holds up.*

High-quality improvements don't just age better—they save you money. Less turnover, fewer repairs, lower cap-ex. And that's cash flow that *stays in your pocket*, not the plumber's.

Longevity isn't about resisting updates—it's about making smart ones that don't fall apart when the wind changes. It's about homes with good bones, smart design, and materials that don't throw in the towel after two tenants and a leaky faucet.

We pulled over under the shade of a big old oak tree, the kind whose roots buckled the sidewalk and had probably been there longer than most of the homes on the block. I let the pen rest against my notebook, the words still fresh:

Cash Flow. Scarcity. Demand. Longevity.

Four words. Four filters. Four ways to see past the sticker price and into the soul of a deal.

My mentor didn't speak right away. He leaned back in his seat, arm draped casually across the steering wheel, as if he had all the time in the world. But I could feel his eyes on me. Watching. Weighing. Not to judge but to see if the lesson had landed.

"Most people," he finally said, "spend their whole lives chasing low prices. Sales. Bargains. They think if they get something cheap, they've won." He gave a little shrug. "But true investors? The ones who last? They're not hunting price. They're hunting value."

He turned slightly toward me, his voice calm but deliberate. "Because price is just noise. It's the number someone's hoping to get. Could be right, could be way off. But value? Value tells you what something *will do* for you. Not just what it costs."

I nodded slowly, still turning the thought over.

He went on. "You remember that watch back at the pawn shop?" I nodded again. "Cheap price. Looked like a deal. But it had been stripped of what gave it value. That's what happens when people chase price. They end up owning something that costs them more

158

than they ever expected because it was missing the pieces that actually gave it value."

I looked back down at my notes, the four words now underlined twice. Anchors.

He pointed a finger toward them.

That right there is how you win over time. Don't ask, *'Can I get it cheap?'* Ask, *'What will this give back to me—year after year?'* Ask, *'Is this a machine I want to own for the next ten years?'*

Because if it's not... then why are you buying it?

The Fifth Filter

A few weeks later, our next meeting didn't happen in front of a house, or at CTU. It happened in a red vinyl booth at a burger joint downtown.

We sat across from each other at a small table, elbows brushing laminated menus, the scent of grilled onions and grease clinging to everything. Between us sat a plate of half-eaten burgers, a pile of property printouts, and my ever-present notebook.

I had just walked my mentor through a deal I felt good about. Really good. It aligned with the four filters we had talked about last time we met.

It was a three-bedroom, two-bath brick ranch on a quiet cul-de-sac. Solid structure, newer roof, and updated kitchen. Rent comps looked strong. There was enough margin for cash flow. Only three homes had sold in that neighborhood in the past six months, and all went under contract in less than a week. School district was improving, a new grocery store had just opened nearby, and there was a hospital expansion breaking ground two exits away.

Best of all, the seller was motivated. He was offering the property at a discount—ten percent below the last comp.

"I think it's a win," I said, tapping the top page of the packet with the back of my pen. "It checks the boxes. Cash Flow. Scarcity. Demand. Longevity. And it's priced right."

He looked down at the paper, scanned the numbers, and gave a small nod. "It's a good house," he said.

I smiled, waiting for confirmation. "So… I should buy it?"

He answered by reaching his pocket and pulling out a small, soft velvet pouch. He untied the drawstring, tipped the contents into his palm, and then placed a single gold coin on the table between us.

I blinked. "We using pirate treasure now?"

He didn't laugh. Just tapped the coin gently with his finger. "How much do you think this is worth right now?"

I glanced at it. "About a grand, I think. Give or take."

"Right," he said. "Now, how many of these would it take to buy that house?"

I looked back down at the listing sheet and did a quick mental calculation. "About three hundred. But with that measure, it's worth about three hundred and thirty."

"Okay. Now think about this: if that same house sold ten years ago for two hundred of these… what changed?"

I shrugged. "The price went up?"

He raised an eyebrow. "Or maybe… the dollar went down."

He stared at me as he turned the coin over in his fingers. "See, this—" he said, holding it up, "this is the final filter I use to

160

measure value. Because this doesn't change. This doesn't get printed into oblivion. It doesn't inflate or deflate depending on interest rates or headlines or elections. It just is. Steady. Predictable. Reliable."

He looked me straight in the eye. "It buys the same number of hamburgers today as it did 50 years ago."

"Dollars on the other hand are a constant moving target." He continued. "They're influenced by fear, speculation, manipulation. They're not a stable reference point. Which makes it incredibly confusing for people to truly understand if something is priced at a good value."

I looked down at the listing again—not in terms of a discount or a comp—but as an exchange. Three hundred ounces of gold for this house. That was the new question: Is this property *worth* three hundred ounces of gold?

Was this deal simply discounted in dollars, or was it actually undervalued?

That was the question I couldn't stop thinking about. I started digging into the actual history of real estate prices measured in gold.

The more I looked, the clearer it became. There was a rhythm to it. A relationship. And the deeper I went, the more confident I became that I had been introduced to something more dependable than a headline or a comp.

Gold wasn't just a shiny coin on the table. It was a key. A baseline. A tool to track real value over time—across cycles, across markets, and across decades.

The Real Story of Gold

Most people today have no idea that for most of American history, our currency wasn't just printed based on political will. It was backed by something real—*gold*. That little yellow metal has been used as a store of value for over 5,000 years. Empires rose and fell on it. Wars were fought over it. Entire civilizations calibrated their economies around it.

And for over a century, the U.S. dollar was tied directly to gold. If you held a paper dollar, you were legally entitled to exchange it for a fixed amount of gold from the U.S. Treasury. That system created discipline. The government *couldn't* print more money than it had gold to back it up.

That model worked well for a while…until it didn't.

In 1933, in the depths of the Great Depression, President Franklin D. Roosevelt signed Executive Order 6102. It made it illegal for American citizens to own gold. Not kidding. People were required—by law—to turn in their gold coins, bars, and bullion to the government.

Why? Because the U.S. was broke. We were still reeling from World War I, and looking down the barrel of World War II, at a time when the Depression had gutted the economy. The government needed more spending power—but they couldn't print more money without the gold to back it. So they took the gold, then revalued it—from $20.67 an ounce to $35 overnight. Just like that, the supply of money expanded more than 70%, without printing a single new ounce of metal.

It was the first bait-and-switch. The first time the American public realized the rules could be changed *after* the game had started.

From there, the foundation of honest money slowly eroded.

By the late 1960s, inflation was beginning to creep in. The dollar was being quietly devalued through inflation—printing money—and the pressure on the gold peg was mounting.

The turning point came in 1971. We were deep into the Vietnam War, and once again…we needed money!

That's when President Richard Nixon stepped in front of the cameras and announced that the U.S. was "temporarily" suspending the convertibility of dollars into gold. In other words, he took us off the gold standard. It was pitched as a short-term solution—but it wasn't. It became permanent.

From that moment forward, the dollar became a *fiat currency*. Meaning: it wasn't backed by anything but faith. No gold. No silver. Just confidence in the U.S. government and its ability to maintain order.

To ensure no one panicked, gold ownership for Americans was still illegal. In fact, it wouldn't be legal to own investment-grade gold until 1974. That's right—there was a 40-year stretch in modern U.S. history where private citizens couldn't legally own the one thing that had held its value for thousands of years.

And that's when the printing really began.

Gold Reveals the Truth

Late one night in my office, years after my mentor planted that initial idea in my head, during the time where I was preparing to unwind my portfolio and move back into single family houses, I started calculating historical home prices in *ounces of gold*. I pulled up data from the Federal Reserve Bank of St. Louis and matched it against gold prices going back decades.

In 1970, gold was $35 an ounce. The median-priced home was $23,900.

680 ounces of gold.

Fast forward to 1980. Gold had exploded to $559 an ounce. Home prices had tripled to $63,000.

113 ounces of gold.

In dollar terms, homes had *tripled*. But in gold terms? They had become 85% *cheaper*.

Why? Because in 1980, no one wanted real estate. Interest rates were hovering around 17%. Owning a house was expensive, and mortgage payments were brutal. Real estate was radioactive.

The gold told the true story. It revealed that even though prices had soared, *value* had plummeted. And suddenly, everything my mentor said made perfect sense.

The dollar was lying to me. Gold was telling the truth. So I kept digging.

Here's what happened in the decades that followed:

- 2007: Gold hits $625/oz.
- 2009: $879/oz.
- 2012: $1,645/oz.
- 2022: $1,769/oz.
- 2025: $3,450/oz.

I couldn't believe what I was seeing! The unbelievable amount of money the US Government was printing was having a very visible, very meaningful impact on inflation. It was undeniable in the price of gold. I went back and compared how many ounces it took to buy the *same* median home at those different moments in recent history.

Here is what it revealed:

- **2007**: Gold was **$625/oz**
  The median U.S. home cost around **$257,400**.
  → That's **412 ounces** of gold.

- **2009**: Gold climbs to **$879/oz**
  Home prices fall to about **$208,400**.
  → Now just **237 ounces**.

- **2013**: Gold hits **$1,645/oz**
  Homes are still near the bottom at **$238,700**.
  → That's **145 ounces**.

- **2022**: Gold at **$1,769/oz**
  Median home price jumps to **$438,000**.
  → That's **247 ounces**.

- **2025**: Gold hits **$3,450/oz**
  The median home price is **$416,900**.
  → That's just **121 ounces**.

Let that last one sink in.

In dollar terms, housing looks like it is continuing to get more expensive. Each year it looks more expensive than ever. The headlines scream about affordability crises, pricing bubbles, and first-time buyers getting priced out of the market. On paper, each new surge feels like we've hit the stratosphere.

But when you step back and view it through the lens of gold, the story changes. Dramatically.

Because in gold terms? Housing isn't more expensive—it's actually cheaper than it's been in decades.

That might sound impossible, but the math doesn't lie. If you go all the way back—through the charts, the data, the archives of the Federal Reserve—you'll see something stunning. From the 1960s through today, the median U.S. home price has historically hovered between 350 to 400 ounces of gold. Sometimes a little higher. Sometimes a little lower. But mostly, it stayed within that range.

Today? It's well below that.

Not because homes have gotten worse.

Not because people stopped needing shelter.

Not because the land has less utility or the brick holds less heat.

No—the homes haven't changed. The measuring stick has.

The dollar isn't just bending—it's unraveling. Quietly. Slowly. In full view of a public that's grown numb to rising numbers and shrinking value.

And if you're still evaluating your investments using a ruler that stretches and shrinks with every economic tremor, then you're chasing shadows. Because the price may go up, but that doesn't mean the value has.

That's the trap.

When I saw that data, something snapped into focus. And what stared back at me wasn't just information—it was an invitation.

It meant real estate was on sale.

Not because the price had dropped in dollars, but because the real value had dropped. Because the asset was being mispriced. Misunderstood.

And in that gap—between price and value—is where every great investor finds their edge.

A Better Way to See Value

We were back at that same burger joint—iced tea in hand, sun cutting through the window blinds—and this time, I had something for him.

I slid my notebook across the table.

"I've been thinking about what you said all those years ago," I told my mentor. "About using gold to measure value."

He didn't say a word, just leaned forward and started flipping through the pages.

I had laid it all out—year by year, data point by data point. Median home prices in dollars. Gold prices by the ounce. And most importantly, the number of ounces it took to buy a house in each era.

I circled the number in red ink. "That's where we are," I said. "Right now."

He traced the line with his finger, then looked up at me with a quiet, satisfied smile. "Now you're seeing it."

And I was. I was no longer just seeing price. I was seeing *value*.

Because price is just noise. It's what the market screams. It's the sticker slapped on the window. But value—that's what whispers beneath the surface. It doesn't care what the headlines say or how the market feels this week. Value is steady. It's fundamental. And when you learn to see it clearly, you stop flinching at prices… and start seeing the truth behind them.

The true value.

Chapter Eight

Money is a Tool

If price is what you pay, and value is what it's worth…
then what is money itself?

Most people cruise through life thinking money *is* the wealth. Earn enough and you're rich. Simple, right?

Except it's dead wrong.

Money isn't the treasure. It isn't even the map to the treasure. Money's the shovel. The hammer. The duct tape you keep in the toolbox because it somehow fixes everything from leaky pipes to broken pride.

Money is a tool.

And like any tool, it's got a very specific purpose. You wouldn't grab a hammer to tighten a bolt or screw in a hinge. That's not what it was made for. Yet that's exactly how most people use money. They swing it at problems it was never designed to solve, and then get frustrated when nothing holds together.

There's nothing wrong with the hammer. There's nothing wrong with the screw. The problem is how you're using the tool. A hammer drives nails, pulls nails—and occasionally smashes stuff when you're mad. That's it.

And money? Same deal. It has two jobs:

- *Money creates incentive.*

- *Money transfers wealth.*

That's all. Everything else we've been told about money—work harder, trade more hours, save enough and you'll be free—is the big lie. You will never be able to trade your time for enough money to become wealthy. You don't have enough time.

Fortunately, there's a better way. A simpler way. And you don't need unlimited piles of cash to do it. You just need to learn how to use the tool properly.

Money Creates Incentive

I remember the day that idea really hit home. It wasn't in a book, or a podcast. It wasn't even standing across from my mentor at CTU – although he had tried to tell me in one of our lessons there. But just hearing the lesson in theory and actually living it out are two very different things.

Which is how I found myself one Saturday, in the middle of repositioning my portfolio. Fixing up and selling the assets I didn't want to hold for the next 10 years. The ones that were squeezing the life out of me.

Back in my old work boots, sleeves rolled up, doing what I knew best: working with my hands. Hanging doors, trimming baseboards, swapping out fixtures—none of it was beyond me. I'd built houses for a living. I was good at this stuff.

And that was the trap.

Because when you know how to swing the hammer, the hammer starts to look like the solution to every problem. My mindset was still stuck in the old playbook: work harder, grind longer, save money by doing it yourself. It made me feel productive, tough, even smart—like I was squeezing more value out of the deal.

But I wasn't saving money.

I was burning time. Hours I could've spent finding the next deal, building new relationships, or just being with my family were being traded away for work I already knew how to do. Work that wasn't moving me forward.

By dinnertime, I was still there—dusty, sweaty, and clinging to the idea that I was somehow being efficient. That's when I heard it: gravel crunching under tires.

I looked up from the baseboard I was nailing down and saw my mentor's truck pull into the driveway. Of course he showed up at just the right moment—like a sitcom character entering stage left to drop wisdom.

He stepped out, sunglasses on, coffee in hand, and leaned on the open truck door like a detective surveying a crime scene. The crime? Me, murdering my Saturday.

"You living here now?" he asked, grinning.

I wiped my hands on my jeans, sheepish and defeated. "Just trying to knock this thing out today."

He nodded slowly. Walked up the steps, studied the new hand railing I'd just installed. Peeked inside. Took a good, long look. Half-painted baseboards, piles of scrap on the floor, open toolboxes strewn across the living room like I'd hosted a hardware-themed yard sale.

Then he turned around, strolled back to his truck, dropped the tailgate with a thunk, and patted the spot next to him.

"Sit," he said. "You look like you could use five minutes."

He was right.

We sat there in silence. The kind of silence that says, *You already know what I'm about to tell you... but I'll let you feel it first.* A squirrel darted across the yard, probably laughing at me. The sun was beginning to dip, that golden hour where the light turns dramatic—like even the sky is disappointed in how you spent your day.

That's when he said it.

"Money is a tool. And you're using it wrong."

I turned to him, squinting like he'd just accused me of eating cereal with a fork. "I'm *saving* money," I said, half-defensive, half-delusional. "I know how to do this work, and I can do it cheaper than hiring someone."

He shook his head, slow and steady, like he was watching someone try to fix a laptop with a hammer.

"No," he said. "You're *burning* time. You're trading the thing you say you're trying to buy—*freedom*—for the illusion of control."

Long pause.

And just when I thought I might wiggle out of the lesson, he piled on.

"Money has two jobs," he said, holding up two fingers like he was ordering at a drive-thru. "Two purposes. First, it creates *incentive*. Incentive for someone else to build wealth *for* you. Pay them. Pay

173

them well. Pay them fast. Give them a reason to bring their best work to *your* machine."

He pointed at the house behind me—the one I'd been treating like a DIY obstacle course. "That house is a machine. Every hour you spend inside swinging a hammer, you're not just getting sweaty— you're slowing down the machine. You're jamming a wrench in the gears. That house was designed to produce income. *Passive* income. *Long-term* income. The kind that doesn't clock out just because you're tired."

I didn't say anything.

I got it—I did. Every word made perfect sense. But when you've built your identity around being the guy who shows up, straps on the tool belt, and figures it out, it's hard to admit that the best move might be... *letting go of the hammer*.

He didn't press. He just kept going, calm as ever.

"Think about it," he said. "You're out here, sweating through your shirt to save a few hundred bucks on labor. But what if that same time—those same hours—could be spent finding the *next* machine? Or building a relationship with a banker who'll fund your next *three*?"

Then he leaned in slightly, just enough to make sure it landed.

"You're the investor," he said. "Your job is to *design* the machine. *Not to be the machine.*"

There was no judgment in his voice. Just clarity. Clarity I desperately needed.

I stood there, paintbrush in hand, looking like a man who'd just lost a boxing match to a ceiling fan.

Physically wrecked. Emotionally spent. Mentally somewhere between *why do I do this* and *is it too late to become a park ranger?*

I had traded an entire day of my life—prime Saturday real estate—for work that someone else could've done faster, better, and probably without getting primer in their hair. Work that didn't require my presence, just my permission and a well-written check.

Up until then, I thought leverage meant borrowing money. That was the only lever I knew—debt.

But people?

People are leverage, too.

And money, properly used, is the lever you pull.

When you pay a contractor to fix up your rental, you're not just covering a labor invoice. You're creating *incentive*. You're pointing talent, skill, and experience directly at your machine and saying, "Go make this better." You're not handing over cash—you're *activating capacity*.

You're not just buying labor.

You're buying *time*.

You're buying *progress*.

You're buying margin. Mental bandwidth. A Saturday that doesn't end with you cursing at closet doors like they moonlight as professional wrestlers who just smacked you down with a folding chair.

You're buying a day with your kids. A moment on the porch. A nap, for crying out loud. But even more than that—you're *accelerating wealth*.

Because every nail driven, every fixture replaced, every coat of paint that actually matches? That's moving the dial. Rent goes up. Expenses dip. Equity rises like dough in a warm kitchen. And suddenly that little machine isn't just humming—it's *roaring*. Spinning faster. Throwing off more cash. Giving you options you didn't have before.

All because you gave someone else a reason to bring their *best* to *your* machine.

Money Transfers Wealth

He let me sit with it. No lecture. No pep talk. Just the quiet sound of drywall dust settling around my bad decisions.

Then he kept going—same tone, same rhythm—like this was all part of one big, clear thought I was finally ready to hear.

"But money's got a second job, too," he said, raising his finger again like he was placing an order for wisdom with a side of fries. "It doesn't just create incentive. It transfers wealth."

I blinked. "Transfers wealth?"

He nodded. "Think about it. Before money, if you had wheat and wanted chickens, you had to find someone who had chickens *and* just happened to be jonesing for a sack of grain. And if Chicken Guy wasn't feeling the wheat? Well, now you're on a side quest. You've gotta trade your wheat for goat cheese, the goat cheese for a barrel of eel oil, the eel oil for a handcrafted lute, and *then* hope you can convince some guy named Bartholomew the Beekeeper to swap that lute for three chickens and a suspiciously aggressive rooster."

He leaned back and grinned. "It was basically a medieval scavenger hunt with livestock and poor time management."

I laughed, shaking my head.

"It's like trying to barter your way through a Renaissance fair run by people who all specialize in one very specific item and absolutely *do not* negotiate. You're seven trades deep just to get breakfast."

I chuckled, wiping construction dust off my arm. "That would have been exhausting!"

He nodded. "It *was* exhausting. You couldn't get anything you needed—or wanted—without growing it, hunting it, or bartering your way through a 12-step trading maze that involved at least one questionable jar of pickled herring."

He glanced toward the house. "Then money showed up and changed that. Suddenly, you didn't need to carry around sacks of barley or hand-knit socks to make a deal. Money became the middleman. A temporary storage container for value. A universal translator for trade. A bridge."

He tapped the side of his water bottle like it was a piggy bank.

"You could sell something today, store that value in the form of money, and wait until you found the *right* thing to buy next. The money wasn't the prize. It was just the tool that let you move value from one asset to another—without needing to juggle chickens and eel oil in the meantime."

He pointed back at the house—the one I had just spent my Saturday wrestling into rent-ready shape.

"That house?" he said. "*That's* the wealth. That's the asset. It printed money for you. When you sell it, it's not because you're cashing out to go buy a jet ski and a midlife crisis. It's because you've got your eye on another machine—newer build, better neighborhood, stronger yield."

He tilted his head. "The money you make from this place? That's not a prize. It's the *transfer case*—just the box you use to carry value from one machine to the next."

He took a slow breath like he was giving my brain a moment to lace up its shoes and catch up.

"Most people don't see it that way," he continued. "They sell a place like this and think the cash is the win. So they celebrate. Upgrade the truck to something that growls when it starts. Install a pizza oven in the backyard like they're auditioning for a reality show called *Wood-Fired Dreams*. Or blow it all on kitchen counters so shiny they could redirect satellites."

I laughed—hard—because I *knew* that guy. I'd seen that exact post on social media: "Just sold my rental! Check out my granite waterfall and new F-350 with mood lighting."

"But what they're really doing?" he said, his tone shifting—funnier moments behind us now. "They're cashing in the machine. Trading a goose that lays golden eggs… for a really fancy omelet. Sure, it tastes great. It's warm, buttery, looks great on Instagram—maybe it even comes with a side of avocado toast and a caption about *living your best life*."

He leaned against his truck and looked me straight in the eye.

"But that omelet?" he said. "It doesn't lay another egg."

And just like that, the noise in my head went quiet.

I hadn't been thinking of the sale as the finish line. Truth is, I hadn't been thinking of the sale at all. Wasn't I just supposed to keep these forever? Build up more doors until the spreadsheet looked impressive?

But now I could see it—sometimes the smart move isn't to hold… it's to *upgrade the machine.*

The house wasn't the goal. The money wasn't the trophy. The sale wasn't an exit—it was a pivot. A handoff. A chance to roll the value forward into something stronger, more efficient, more aligned with the future I was actually trying to build.

Freedom wasn't hiding in the pile of cash.

"The money," he said finally, "isn't the wealth. The money is the *tool.* In this case? It's a wheelbarrow."

He motioned like he was rolling one up a plank. "You load it with the results of one machine, cart it across the job site, and dump it straight into the foundation of the next. Sell the asset. Transfer the value. Build something stronger. Money's just how you *move* the wealth—not where it lives."

I looked down at my hands—still covered in paint, caulk, and at least two types of regret—but for the first time all day, I didn't feel like a guy who was patching holes. I felt like a guy who was *making progress.*

Not just spinning in circles. *Building forward.*

He capped his water bottle, stood tall, and gave the house one last glance—the kind of look a builder gives when he knows the job is done, but the work's not over.

"Most people sell the machine to buy comfort," he said. "A fancier lifestyle. Softer seats. Shinier toys. But the ones who build real wealth?"

He paused, just long enough for it to land.

"They use the sale to buy *time*."

My mentor turned and looked me dead in the eye.

"You can hustle your way into a few houses," he said. "But if you want real wealth—*freedom* wealth—you've gotta start building machines that don't require you to crank the gears by hand."

Then he added, with the kind of calm certainty that makes you feel both inspired and lightly rebuked:

"That's how smart investors think. Money doesn't sit. It moves. It motivates. It *multiplies*."

He nodded toward the house, now littered with my exhaustion and misplaced pride.

"You'll get more of those built," he said, "if you're not the one inside hanging doors."

And just like that, he climbed back into his truck and drove off—the crunch of gravel behind him fading like the tail end of a sermon you didn't realize you needed.

Paying it Forward

A few years later, I found myself behind the wheel on a long drive home from Florida. My son was in the passenger seat, half-buried in a bag of Cheetos, half-lost in his own thoughts. You know, that magical age where they oscillate between Zen monk silence and philosophical depth that would make Socrates blink. The road was long, the snacks were dwindling, and the silence between playlists was thick enough to spread on a cracker.

Then, from the passenger seat, came the ambush.

"Dad, what would you do if you had unlimited money?"

I laughed. Not at him—at the memory of myself asking the same kind of question, back when I thought the answer to everything was a bigger pile of cash.

"I wouldn't want unlimited money," I smiled.

He gave me a look like I'd just said I hated pizza. "What? Come on, Dad. Unlimited money. No limits. What would you do?"

Now, I knew what he wanted—he wanted me to hop on the fantasy train, ride it all the way to the golden station where Lamborghinis are free and ice cream is a food group. But this was a mentor moment dressed in Cheeto dust. So instead of boarding the train, I flipped the tracks.

"Alright," I said. "But let's back it up. Why would you want unlimited money?"

He didn't hesitate. His eyes lit up like a squirrel spotting an unguarded bird feeder. "So I could have money to make movies and never stress out about bills. I could travel, live in an awesome house, hang with friends, do whatever I want—all without ever worrying about work or money."

I nodded. He wasn't chasing money. Like most people he was describing freedom.

"You don't need unlimited money to do that, son." I said. "You just need to understand what money really is. Money isn't the treasure. It's not freedom. It's the tool. And it only has two jobs: it creates incentive, and it transfers wealth."

He went quiet. I could see the gears turning, eyes on the road, brain chewing on something bigger than Cheetos. In that silence, reflecting back to sitting on my mentor's tailgate, I felt it—the shift.

I wasn't just the student anymore. I wasn't just the guy swinging a hammer on Saturdays, or even the one listening to wisdom on a truck tailgate. I was the one passing it on.

That's how I knew the lesson had finally landed. Not when I first heard it. Not even when I lived it. But when I could hand it down. Because that's the cycle my mentor expected: you listen with a teachable spirit, then you take action and use the lesson, and then to truly achieve mastery—you teach the lesson.

It was my turn to pay it forward. To teach the lessons to the next generation.

Chapter Nine

How Money Really Works

Money isn't minted; it's manufactured. Watch the machine, buy for cash flow, and let dilution grow your assets—not your grocery bill.

We were sitting on a shaded bench outside a bank downtown. It was our standing weekly meeting. I was deep into executing my plan to simplify my life and buy my time back. A process that caused me to keep thinking further ahead and ask more questions.

"Here's what keeps me up," I said, sliding my phone into my pocket. "We've talked about price versus value. I understand the concept of using gold as my measuring stick. But what happens if the government just keeps printing more dollars? What happens then?"

The corners of his mouth tugged into a grin. He had been waiting for this question so we could talk about how money really works. How it is created, what it really is, how it enters the system and moves into the economy. *This is the core of the rigged system.* The one designed to keep you broke if you don't understand the rules.

"There's no *what if* about it," he said. "They absolutely will. It's how the system works. How it's designed."

"This is the most important lesson of all to truly building wealth, and it's also the part almost no one thinks about." He leaned forward, lowering his voice like he was letting me in on the world's worst magic trick. "Everyone's so distracted by political rhetoric and policies, interest rates and taxes. Things they get mad about and protest over. Meanwhile they miss the one thing in this whole rigged system that is truly keeping them broke: the money supply is going to expand. Always."

I dropped my head. "Inflation."

He nodded slowly, like a teacher glad the student had finally caught the scent. "Exactly."

How Money is Created

He set his coffee on the bench between us and drew a little invisible sketch in the air with his finger.

"When the government needs money, they don't crack open some savings vault. They have the Treasury print a bond. A beautifully engraved IOU. A promise. 'Lend us money now, we'll pay you later—with interest.'"

He paused, then flicked his hand in the other direction. "And over at the Federal Reserve? Same thing. They print a similarly elaborate piece of paper with beautiful designs, but a different name: the dollar. Also created out of nothing."

I narrowed my eyes, following him closely.

He smiled again. "Then they swap. The Treasury hands the Fed a bond. The Fed hands the Treasury brand-new dollars. Ta-da! Money appears."

"Printed out of thin air," I muttered.

"Well, sort of. People imagine money as vaults of cash, armored trucks, or gold bars stacked like Lego bricks. But that's a fantasy.

Most of our currency today is just created digitally, printed on a computer screen with the press of a button." he corrected. "But, essentially, yes. It's created out of thin air."

I sat back against the bench. "So all the dollars in existence are actually owed back to the Fed?"

His smile faded to something closer to solemn. "At their root, yes. But our financial system is also designed to expand the base money supply through our banking and credit systems. We'll talk about that in a minute. First, let's look at the base money that is created. It's called M1 currency."

He reached into his pocket and pulled out his phone. A few taps, then he held it up.

US Currency Supply

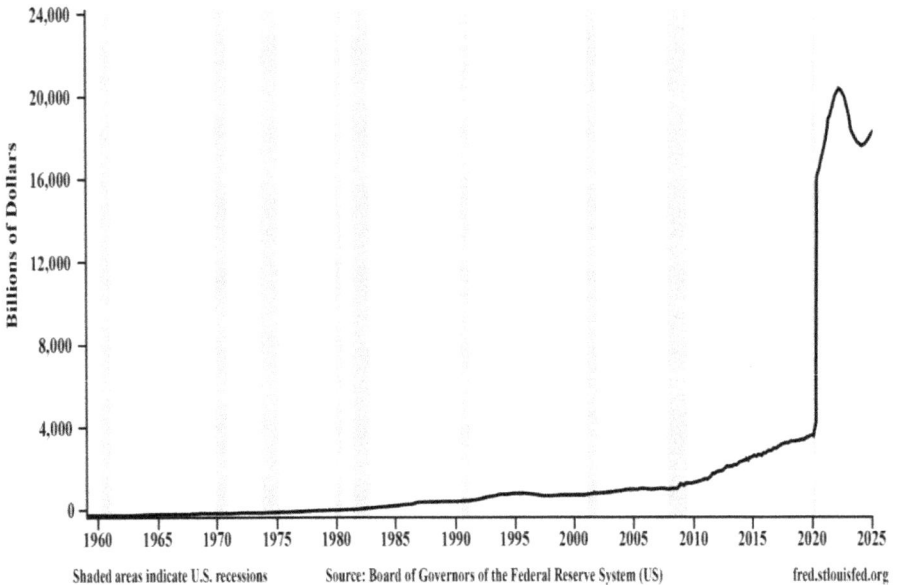

Shaded areas indicate U.S. recessions   Source: Board of Governors of the Federal Reserve System (US)   fred.stlouisfed.org

Source: https://fred.stlouisfed.org/series/M1SL#

"This is the M1 money supply. Think of it as money that you can actually spend: cash, checking account and savings account deposits. Notice anything odd about this chart?" he asked.

The beginning of the chart looked stable—a slow, steady climb across decades. Then, out of nowhere, it rocketed straight up like a bottle rocket in 2020. For a second, I thought it was a glitch. It wasn't. It was a party, where the money was the punch bowl, and the drunk guy who took over as the bar tender was the government.

This is the dark side to the system. The side the government works hard to hide, measuring inflation in a way that allows them to say, "it's under control." The harsh reality is, every time more dollars are created, the ones you've already earned lose strength. And that trend is accelerating.

He slipped the phone away.

I let the words hang while traffic rolled by. The groceries that cost more, the rent that crept higher, the savings that seemed to drain like water through your fingers—all of it tied back to the same truth:

We're living in a world made of Funny Money.

The Rise (and Reinventions) of the Dollar

We left the bench and strolled down the sidewalk, our conversation stretching past storefronts and old brick banks that had seen more than a century of financial history. My mentor gestured toward a mural—an old map of the United States painted on the side of a building, railroads streaking across farmland, rivers carving through wilderness.

"Our money didn't work that way back then," he said, nodding at the mural, "Back then there wasn't just one singular U.S. dollar. Not the way we think of it today. Every bank issued its own currency. The Bank of New York had its notes. So did the Bank of Charleston. Even tiny outfits like the Bank of Augusta printed their own."

It sounded absurd to me, but also familiar—like the Wild West version of Monopoly night. You could win big if your notes held value… or lose everything if they didn't. Merchants had to keep massive ledgers just to keep track of which banknotes were real, which were fake, and which were barely worth the paper. When a bank collapsed—which happened often—its notes became worthless overnight.

It was chaos. And chaos, my mentor reminded me, is always the mother of reform.

In 1913, the U.S. finally tried to tame the system by creating one central bank. The Federal Reserve. A monopoly on the printing of money. It didn't solve every problem, but it gave the nation what it desperately lacked: structure. For the first time, there was one unified dollar instead of thousands of unique ones.

That was the first reinvention of the dollar.

The second came in 1944, when the world gathered at Bretton Woods, New Hampshire, to rebuild the global financial system after World War II. Forty-four allied nations agreed to make the U.S. dollar the world's reserve currency. Why us? Why the Dollar? Because at the time, America owned more than 60% of the world's gold. If other nations pegged their money to the dollar, and the dollar was pegged to gold at $35 an ounce, everyone could trust the system.

It was elegant—a neat little triangle of faith. For a while, it worked.

But by the 1960s, America had been writing checks it didn't have the gold to cash. Wars, social programs, and expansion had the printing presses running faster than the vaults could keep up. Other countries noticed. Nervous, they started demanding gold in exchange for their dollars. In 1965, France even sent a warship across the Atlantic to haul gold back home.

That pressure led to the third reinvention of the dollar. You may remember, we talked about this briefly before when we discussed using gold to determine value. In August 1971, Nixon went on television and announced that the U.S. would "temporarily" suspend the dollar's convertibility into gold. But temporary in government-speak is like saying the "diet starts Monday"—it never came back. The dollar was permanently cut loose from the gold standard.

From that day forward, money was no longer tied to anything solid. No anchor. No gold. Just trust and confidence.

It was a moment most people didn't fully grasp the significance of at the time—but it reshaped the entire world. For the first time, the dollar became what it is today: a pure fiat currency. Backed only by the full faith and credit of the US Government.

And here's the irony. The Federal Reserve was created in 1913 to prevent panics and bring stability. But by 1971, it had evolved into something far more powerful. It wasn't just a referee anymore; it had become the player that controlled the game itself. With no gold standard to restrain it, the Fed had the freedom to print, contract, or manipulate the money supply at will.

That was the beginning of the modern age of Funny Money.

The Modern Money Machine

By the time we turned off Broad Street and headed toward the river, I thought the history lesson was over. But my mentor wasn't done. He slowed his pace, and I could tell he was choosing his next words carefully.

"After 1971," he said, "there was nothing left to restrain the Fed. No gold. No hard anchor. Just policy. From then on, every time the economy caught a cold, the prescription was the same: easier money. Pour more booze in the punch bowl." And for a while, it worked.

Then came 2008.

I remembered that one personally. It wasn't just a headline—it was something I felt in my life, in my portfolio. It almost crushed me and forced me out of the game, back to framing houses for a living. The collapse started with subprime loans and mortgage-backed securities, but it spread like wildfire. Banks failed. Lending froze. The stock market lost half its value.

And for the Fed, that was the moment the modern money machine kicked into high gear.

"They called it quantitative easing," my mentor said. "A polite term for what it really was: dumping more liquor into the punch bowl. Printing trillions of dollars to buy toxic assets, bail out banks, and flood the system with cash."

We watched housing prices soar in real time during the next market expansion, not because the houses suddenly got better, but because the supply of cheap money exploded. Cheap debt became the new gold rush. Zero-percent rates made capital flow like water, and asset prices ballooned. Stocks, bonds, housing—all rising, not because they were creating more value, but because the Fed was creating more dollars.

It solved the immediate problem. But it also taught a dangerous lesson: that the Fed could pump trillions into the economy without immediate catastrophe. Like giving a diabetic just enough insulin to stay alive—while feeding him donuts the whole time.

The monetary base in 2008 was under $900 billion. By 2020, it had ballooned to nearly $4 trillion.

And then 2020 hit—COVID.

US Currency Supply

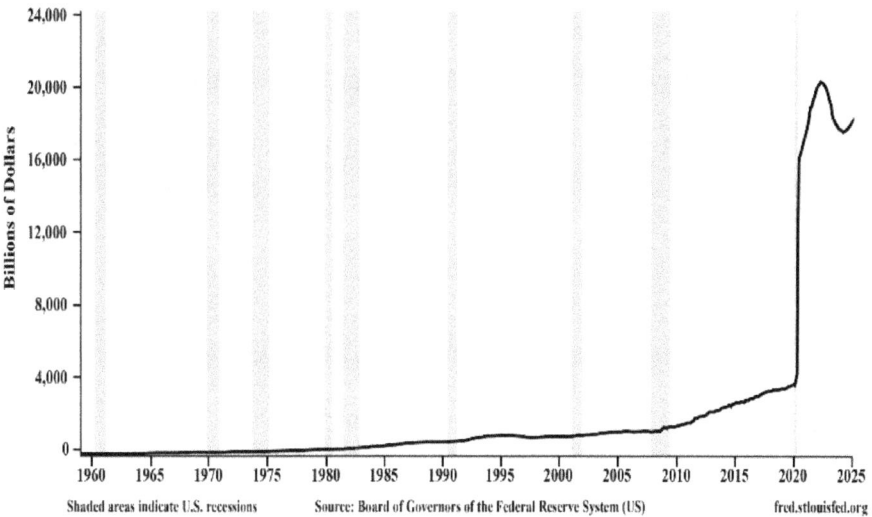

Shaded areas indicate U.S. recessions   Source: Board of Governors of the Federal Reserve System (US)   fred.stlouisfed.org

The government shut down the economy. The Fed turned the firehose on full blast. Over $17 trillion was injected into the financial system between 2020 and 2022. Stimulus checks, PPP loans, corporate bailouts, direct injections into markets. It was like opening a fire hydrant in the middle of a drought and calling it rain.

From the sidewalk, we stopped to look out at the skyline. The buildings stood the same as they always had, but underneath, the foundation of the financial system had shifted.

"That's the modern machine," he said. "It doesn't run on savings anymore. It runs on credit and printed money. And every time the market twitches, the Fed doesn't just referee. It plays."

That realization rewired the way I invest. There is no doubt, fundamentals still matter—they keep you grounded. But the Fed is controlling the game. So now, I keep one eye on the three major cycles—the P-cycle, N-cycle and M-cycle, and the other eye focused squarely on the money supply. Because when the Fed floods the system, assets float. When it pulls back, they sink.

"That," he said, finishing my thought, "is the real game investors have to learn now. Not just watching property values, but watching the money."

The Mandrake Mechanism: How Banks Multiply Money

We crossed into a wide plaza, the kind of space that hosted farmer's markets in the summer and empty echoes in the winter. All of this was blowing my mind.

"So, you said earlier that after the Fed creates the money, the banks expand it? What do you mean by that?" I asked.

"The Federal Reserve is only the spark." He replied. "The real bonfire comes from the banks themselves."

It's called fractional reserve banking—and it's all part of our rigged system. A system that makes Mandrake the Magician look like an amateur card trickster. The simple explanation of this is: for every dollar the Fed creates and pushes into the economy, nine more are created through our banking system.

Here's how it works. Say you deposit $1,000 in your checking account. Most people think the bank tucks it away like grandma hiding cash in a cookie jar, waiting patiently until you need it again. Not even close. In reality, the bank is only required to keep a small fraction of that money in reserves—historically around 10%. The other $900? It gets lent out.

But here's the kicker: once that $900 lands in someone else's account, *their* bank only has to keep 10% too. So it holds onto $90 and lends out $810. That cycle repeats again and again. One deposit becomes a series of loans, and by the time the dust settles, your original $1,000 has multiplied into nearly $10,000 of "money" circulating in the system.

Not printed. Not mined. Just conjured.

That's the Mandrake Mechanism—money multiplied through lending, disappearing and reappearing like a magician's coin trick. Except instead of coins, we get houses, cars, and credit card balances.

In boom times, this system feels like rocket fuel. Capital flows easily. Credit is cheap. Everyone's flush. Developers build. Families borrow. Banks lend. And the illusion works—until it doesn't.

Because the same way the money supply is expanded through lending, it disappears when loans go bad. When people default, that multiplied money doesn't just freeze—it vanishes. Like someone pulling bricks out of the foundation, piece by piece.

That's why contractions happen so brutally fast. A single default doesn't just erase one loan; it unravels all the multiplied dollars tied to it. Suddenly the money supply contracts, banks tighten, lending dries up, and the boom turns into bust.

It's not a conspiracy. It's not even a mistake. It's a mechanical truth. Credit-based money is fragile. It exists only as long as people keep paying.

Which is why smart investors don't build their fortunes on hope and borrowed air. They prepare for both directions of the money cycle. They don't overleverage. They buy hard assets, like real estate that produce cash flow. They maintain liquidity. They understand that every expansion already has its contraction baked in.

The Mandrake Mechanism isn't just a parlor trick or a scam. It's the heartbeat of modern finance.

No National Debt equals No Money?

We walked in silence drifting through downtown. I was turning the lesson over in my mind like it was a magician's coin, looking at the other side. Trying to see the magic trick he had shown me.

Finally, I said it out loud: "If dollars are created through borrowing, then what happens when the government just pays back the loan?"

He reached into his coat pocket, pulled out a folded bill, and held it up. The edges were frayed, the paper soft from years of being carried like it had been in his wallet for decades. "Great question," he said. "That's why I say this isn't wealth. It's an IOU with fancy artwork. It even says it right there: *Federal Reserve Note.* A note is just debt wearing a tuxedo."

Think about it. Debt is what happens when you don't have enough money to pay your bills. So, you borrow money and go into debt. It's the same thing for the government. When they need money to fund projects, or pump money into the economy, they borrow it.

That means new money is created when the government doesn't have enough...which is pretty much every year. They borrow more of it by printing it, which means every year they take on more debt. The reality is, money only exists because debt exists. When they pay back the bonds—the loans, it erases the government debt, and the dollars vanish right along with it."

I paused to think about what he just said. It was a little confusing at first. "So, all the talk about 'eliminating the national debt'…that would also eliminate all our money?"

He chuckled. "Exactly. If the government took all the money back that it has put into circulation and paid off all the bonds it issued, there would be no more dollars in circulation. The idea that we could eliminate the debt is either ignorant… or the kind of thing politicians say when they're running for office and need a ten-second sound bite."

"You can reduce the *deficit*—slow down how much extra is being created and put into circulation each year, which would then slow inflation. But eliminating the debt entirely?" He shook his head. "That'd be like draining all the blood from the patient because you're worried about cholesterol. The campaign slogan sounds heroic, but the patient doesn't make it off the table."

We kept walking. The city noise faded into background static.

"So the national debt isn't a flaw in the system," I said, piecing it together. "It *is* the system. The foundation the whole thing is built on."

He gave me a look—not the patient teacher's look I remembered from years ago, but the look of someone who knew the kid didn't need training wheels anymore.

The United States is Not Going Broke

The walk back toward the truck gave me time to let it all settle. It was the perfect backdrop for the conversation that hung in the air: the national debt. Thirty trillion dollars and counting.

"Well, if that's the case, won't we eventually go bankrupt?" I asked.

Most people talk about it like a maxed-out credit card. Cable news anchors spin doomsday scenarios about China repossessing the White House or the Capitol being auctioned off to the highest bidder. It's great television—but it's not real.

Here's the truth: the largest holder of U.S. government debt isn't China. It isn't Japan. It's us—the U.S. government itself. Specifically, the Federal Reserve and federal trust funds like Social Security. The whole thing works like a closed loop.

The Treasury prints bonds. The Federal Reserve buys them in exchange for dollars. Then the Treasury pays interest on those bonds. In some years that interest tops a hundred billion dollars—which sounds terrifying, until you realize the Fed only keeps about seven billion for operating costs and then sends the rest right back to the Treasury.

It's like paying yourself rent on your own house. The loop never really breaks.

That's why America isn't going to default tomorrow morning. The national debt isn't a ticking time bomb in the way people imagine.

It isn't a flaw in the system—it *is* the system. Dollars are born from debt. Remove the debt, and you don't just shrink the money supply, you erase it entirely.

The real danger is not default, it's dilution, aka inflation. Every time the government covers interest payments by creating new money, it waters down the value of every dollar already in circulation. It's the economic equivalent of adding gallons of hot water to a pot of soup—keep stretching it and eventually all you've got left is bland broth.

And who suffers most from that dilution? Not Wall Street. They surf the waves. The people who pay are savers, retirees on fixed incomes, and anyone who still believes that a dollar saved is a dollar earned. They're the ones losing flavor in that watered-down soup.

That's why we shouldn't obsess over the big scary number plastered across headlines. Thirty trillion is shocking, sure, but it's the wrong thing to fear. The real enemy isn't the size of the debt. It's the slow, quiet erosion of purchasing power. It doesn't make breaking news, but it eats away at everything—groceries, rent, savings accounts, futures.

Breaking Free of the Rigged System

As I climbed back into my truck I was energized, it had been a long lesson that day. But I realized it was the piece that brought it all together for me. I had clarity.

There is no doubt, the system is rigged. It's designed to keep you broke if you don't know the rules. Inflating your purchasing power away. Stuck in the trap, trading your time for money that is losing value every day. Chasing stuff—trying to impress people.

The real goal is freedom. Freedom is wealth. And you can break free. You can build a life where you are free. It's out here, waiting for you.

Chapter Ten

Breaking Free!

I was gripping the tiller like it owed me money, and my wife was clinging to the trampoline netting with the wide-eyed intensity of someone trying to survive a theme park ride operated by a toddler on espresso.

It was our first time sailing. Ever.
So naturally, we entered a regatta – a sailing race.

Three tiny catamarans. Three couples with zero experience. One loosely agreed-upon racecourse. Out to the edge of Pigeon Island and back, and absolutely no rules. What unfolded on that crystal-clear bay looked less like a race and more like a high-stakes demolition derby—if the drivers were blindfolded, seasick, and had just read "Sailing for Dummies" on the plane ride over.

We weren't so much sailing as we were participating in a team-building exercise for slightly intoxicated flamingos. We zigged when we should've zagged. Collisions were narrowly avoided. At one point, one guy tacked so violently he flung his wife into the sea. But we laughed the whole time.

To any bystander watching from shore, we probably looked like a mating ritual between confused sea turtles. But for us? It was magic.

When we finally steered our water-worn chariots back to shore, we collapsed into a pair of lounge chairs tucked under the shade of a palm-frond umbrella, laughing so hard we couldn't speak. The warm Caribbean breeze rustled the palms above us. The volcanic cliffs to the left glowed gold in the late sun. Pigeon Island stood watch to the right, wrapping around the bay like a natural armrest. And beyond that, the open water stretched out toward a horizon dusted with island peaks.

That's when the realization came full circle. Back to where the dream began, hammer in hand on a construction site.

This is what I was chasing. Not the money. Not the "stuff". Not even the properties.

I was chasing Freedom. Real freedom.

That's what I felt on that beach, a cold drink sweating in my hand, toes buried in the sand, the laughter of new friends still drifting on the breeze. The chaos of our regatta had left us breathless and smiling. In that moment, we weren't chasing perfection. We were just soaking it all in.

And for the first time in years... I felt completely free.

No clients waiting. No emails pinging. No contractors calling with urgent questions. My phone wasn't even on me. It was somewhere back at the cabana, probably dead—and I couldn't have cared less. There was no rush, no schedule, no pressure. Just a horizon full of islands and a gentle reminder of what life could look like when you finally build the thing you were meant to build.

This—*this*—was what I had been chasing all along.

Freedom.

Not the surface-level, Instagram-filtered version with rented jets and "rise and grind" captions. Not the fantasy where you pretend to be rich for a weekend, so the world thinks you've made it. I'm talking about real freedom.

The kind where you wake up because your body says it's time—not because your alarm does. The kind where your days are filled with things that matter, not tasks you've learned to tolerate. Where you can say "yes" to coaching your kid's soccer team, and "no" to meetings that drain the life out of you. Where you can choose to build, explore, contribute—or even work—but only because you want to, not because your bills say you have to.

That kind of freedom isn't locked behind some velvet rope. It's not reserved for trust fund heirs, influencers, or some elite club. It lives out here, in the real world. It's available. And it's closer than most people realize.

Forward Focus: Prepare for the Future

Years ago, sitting on that beach in St. Thomas I received the existential gut punch that ended up reshaping my entire trajectory. My mentor said something I'll never forget:

"You're chasing the wrong thing. Money is not wealth," he said. "Freedom is wealth."

At the time, I nodded like I understood him. But I didn't fully grasp what he was saying until this moment. The pieces fit together now. Money *wasn't* wealth. It was a tool, multiplied in good times, erased in bad. It wasn't backed by gold or savings, only by confidence and policy. The one guarantee was that the supply would keep expanding, no matter which party was in office or who was sitting in the Fed's big leather chair.

And that realization is critical for breaking free.

I used to think the game was about chasing dollars, earning more of them, protecting them in neat little piles like a dragon hoarding gold. But today I have clarity. Dollars aren't the treasure. They're the tool to building real lasting wealth. The thing that really matters is what I *own*. The hard assets that produce cash flow for me whether I am working or not. Houses that will still be standing if the dollar stumbles. Properties that can't be printed with a keystroke.

Because inflation doesn't punish everyone the same way. It punishes the ones who freeze—the saver who waits for "normal" to return, the retiree stuck on a fixed income, the investor clutching paper while its value leaks away one drip at a time.

But the ones who move? They win. The ones who buy when others are scared, who step forward when the headlines scream fear—they're the ones who come out ahead. Not because they predict the future, but because they prepare for it.

That's the lesson my mentor was telling me I needed to learn.

I'd spent so much of my life trying to *prove* something. I wore hustle like a badge of honor. Working harder than anyone. Pushing every limit. Trying to earn enough to feel safe. Secure. Accomplished.

The reality is, I wasn't getting closer to freedom. I was really building a trap. I was sprinting after money and hoping it would lead to freedom. Still caught in the myth that the hustle and more money would set me free.

Freedom doesn't come from working harder.

And it doesn't come from trading time for *Funny Money*.

The path to freedom isn't complicated, it's just not advertised. Most of us were handed the same outdated plan. We were taught to chase a paycheck, save what's left, and hope that someday—maybe—we'll have enough to stop working. That's not a plan. That's a stall tactic. A polite way of saying, *"Hang in there, maybe retirement won't suck."*

The Solution

There *is* a better way. A better way to build a life that offers more than that. A better way to create a life where income isn't tied to effort. Where our value isn't measured in hours. Where the machines you build—real estate investments—keep working even when you don't.

And you don't need to wait for the right time, or the perfect plan, or someone else's approval.

Right now, in this very moment, you are standing at the threshold of something extraordinary. A window of opportunity. A chance not just to improve your life—but to transform your future. To change your story.

This isn't a pep talk.

This is the fork in the road. A decision point.

There has never been, and there will never be, a more powerful moment—a better moment—than *right now* to buy your first, or your next, investment property.

Not yesterday. Not tomorrow. Today.

During the previous binge of printing *Funny Money,* our government went on a drunken bender and tripled our currency supply. Doubling asset prices over a period of 12 years.

This time around, our government has once again increased the size of the punch bowl and massively inflated our currency supply. Only they did it this time over a period of just 2 ½ years. And they go on TV proclaiming there is no inflation. It's a lie. And this is not the last time this pattern will repeat. It *is* the system.

It takes time for all that new *Funny Money* to ripple through the economy. At first, it shows up in goods and services—groceries, gas, rent. Then it hits asset prices—homes, stocks, collectibles.. Finally, it shows up in wages (if we're lucky).

All of which could have devastating effects for the poor and middle class. Hopefully I am wrong about this. Hopefully our government can actually navigate this tsunami they have created. Time will tell.

NOW is the Time

We can't stop the tsunami. We can't rewrite the rules. We can only understand what the rules are and play the hand we are dealt.

The great news is: It's always a great time to buy real estate if you know what you're doing. If you understand the cycles, you don't freeze when the headlines scream "uncertainty." You see the patterns for what they are—waves. You already know that opportunities exist in every phase of the market. The trick is knowing when to paddle out and prepare to catch the next wave.

That's what the three cycles have given you. They're not just theory; they're a set of lenses that cut through the fog. You can tell when a market is set to lift, when a neighborhood is on the verge of change, and when a property will quietly deliver returns long after the excitement has faded. Most people guess. You don't have to.

And right now, the signals are clear. The next set of waves are already building.

Measured in *Funny Money*, things may feel expensive—but dollars are unreliable. They bend, they shrink, they get nervous. Measure with something stable to see what real value is. Often, the noise says, "too high," while the truth says "on sale."

Meanwhile, the system is still doing what it's always done: creating more *Funny Money* and letting value leak from every bill. Inflation isn't a theory; it's policy. Waiting doesn't protect you—it simply gives the rigged system more time to work against you.

If you understand the rules of the game, you realize this isn't just "a good time" to act. Now is the *best* time to act.

This is the kind of moment where, years from now, people will look back and say, "If only I'd started then."

You've spent your whole life inside a system rigged to keep you broke—trading time for *Funny Money*, saving *Funny Money* that loses value, and being told to "wait for the right moment" while the right moments pass you by.

That ends here. You know the rules now. You know how to play the game. And the next move is yours.

If you've been watching from the sidelines, wondering when to make your move—this is it. If you've been waiting for the perfect plan, the right timing, or a sign from the universe—this is it. You don't need permission. You need conviction. The same kind my mentor handed me, not with a shove, but with a steady hand and quiet truths.

Go buy a house.

Buy one. Fix it up perfectly, rent it out and let someone else pay it off for you over time. When it is paid for, you keep collecting rent.

Then imagine what happens when you do that two or three times. Or maybe you really cut loose and buy five over the next five years.

How many of them do you need to live an amazing life? To retire?

It's not 100!

It's only a few. Just a handful of average homes can replace an average income. That's the path to wealth, freedom and legacy. And you don't have to buy them all at once. In fact, you shouldn't. You should buy them slowly, one at a time.

If you are like I was when I started investing, I didn't have a lot of money. Truthfully, I didn't have any. And the daunting idea that it would take 20 years to pay them off was a lot. Maybe even a little de-motivating.

But 20 years is coming…whether you do anything or not.

So, get started. Start crossing thresholds. Start looking at rocks so you'll know the gold when you see it.

You can close this book, nod, and wait for "someday". Or you can take what you've learned, put your feet on the ground, and start building wealth in a system rigged to keep you broke.

Now is the time.

Go Buy Houses.

www.ingramcontent.com/pod-product-compliance
Lightning Source LLC
Chambersburg PA
CBHW020155200326
41521CB00006B/370